IS THE UNITED STATES MENTIONED IN BIBLE PROPHECY?

With a Treatise on the Ezekiel 38 and Psalm 83 Wars

— 2nd Edition —

Paul R. Wild

To contact the author for speaking engagements
or for additional book purchases:

http://www.TheTimingOfTheRapture.com

Paul R. Wild

P.O. Box 218321

Houston, TX 77218

IS THE UNITED STATES MENTIONED IN BIBLE PROPHECY?

Copyright © 2017 Paul R. Wild

All rights reserved. No part of this publication may be reproduced, stored in a retrieval system, or transmitted in any form or by any means—electronic, mechanical, photocopying, recording, or otherwise—without the prior written permission of the publisher and copyright owner. The only exception is brief quotations in printed reviews.

7710-T Cherry Park Drive, Suite 224
Houston, TX 77095
(281) 830-8724

http://www.WorldwidePublishingGroup.com

Printed in the United States of America

Softcover: 978-1-387-03484-0

Hardcover: 978-1-387-03485-7

Table of Contents

SUMMARY (The Cut to the Chase) 1

> To aid readers who need a simple, straight-forward statement of the issue, the major points are summarized to support the idea that the United States, Great Britain, Russia, and Asian nations such as China are identified by a correct understanding of symbolical beasts in Daniel 7. The invitation is made to those readers who want to study the issue in greater depth to proceed on to subsequent chapters.

MAJOR POINTS 7

> The controversy of whether or not the United States can be found in Bible prophecy is presented, with a summation of the various viewpoints and a brief analysis of the Daniel 7 beasts that symbolize modern nations, including the United States.

IS THE UNITED STATES MENTIONED IN BIBLE PROPHECY? 15

> The chapters in Daniel that focus on prophecies about ancient and modern nations are introduced.

Daniel 2 17

> The statue of King Nebuchadnezzar's dream is detailed to reveal the classical and new viewpoints on the progression of ancient nations predicted by the statue's anatomy. The controversy between the classical position and the new Shoebat/Richardson position regarding replacing the Roman Empire with the Muslim Ottoman Empire is discussed. Theories on the antichrist also are elucidated briefly.

Daniel 4 21

> King Nebuchadnezzar's tree dream is explained regarding his kingdom and his lapse into insanity, followed by repentance and restoration. This pattern has ramifications for understanding the fate of the United States, as explained in the Good News chapter.

Daniel 5 22

The writing on the wall at King Belshazzar's party is translated by Daniel to inform the king of his impending overthrow by the Medes and the Persians.

Daniel 8 23

An angelic being explains Daniel's vision of the Persian and Median ram and the Greek goat, from which spring the kingdoms of Alexander the Great and his four generals, from whose remnant kingdoms the antichrist arises.

Daniel 11 24

Similar to Daniel 8, an angelic being explains Daniel's vision about the Medo-Persian kings leading up to Alexander and his generals, followed by the wars between two generals' families, the Seleucids and the Ptolemys. The Jewish Maccabees are introduced, then the Romans, then the antichrist. The point is made that these kingdoms are known, in contrast to the kingdoms presented in Daniel 7.

Daniel 7 27

The primary subject of this book is expounded upon through detailed analyses of Daniel 7's four beasts.

The First Beast – The Anglo-American Lion with Eagle's Wings 34

Justification is provided for boldly proclaiming that the United States and Great Britain are identified by the lion with eagle's wings.

The Second Beast – The Russian Bear with Turkish, Syrian, and Iranian Ribs 36

Justification is provided for boldly proclaiming that Russia, Turkey, Iran, and Syria compose the bear with three ribs in its mouth.

The Third Beast – The Four-Winged, Four-Headed Asian Leopard 44

Justification is provided for boldly proclaiming that China, India, Japan, and the Koreas compose the leopard with four heads and four wings.

CURRENT EVENTS 47

A discussion of current events is presented that supports the "US is in Bible prophecy" position, including recent media headlines.

GOOD NEWS 59

The textual clues of Daniel 4 and 7 are examined to show that the United States will experience spiritual renewal, revival, and restoration.

THE EZEKIEL 38-39 AND PSALM 83 WARS 63

The connection between the Ezekiel 38-39 and Psalm 83 wars is revealed, with an explanation that they are pre-Tribulation wars that lead to the introduction of the antichrist. The idea that the Ezekiel 38-39 war provides support for the Daniel 7 "modern nations" viewpoint is exposited. The Day of the Lord and its prophetical significance is also explained.

APPENDIX A - RECENT EVENTS SINCE JUNE 2011 85

An informal compendium of supporting information for the "US is in Bible prophecy" position is presented, covering the period from June to October 2011, after the publication of the first edition of this book.

US Decline.. 85

Topics include Russian and Chinese advancements, economic decay, cultural decay, natural and political disasters, etc.

Psalm 83/Middle East War 95

Topics include Israel's increasing isolation by the global community and the activities of Muslim terrorists.

APPENDIX B – DAY OF THE LORD 99

A compendium of Scripture passages is presented regarding the Day of the Lord.

SUMMARY (The Cut to the Chase)

If you really want to cut to the chase, the short answer to the question posed on the book cover is, "Yes."

I began work on the first edition of this book in 2009 and completed it in June 2011. Of the handful of people who have read it and cared to provide me feedback, the consensus is that I've made a compelling case that the US is identified in Scripture. Some even fully adopted my position. Nevertheless, they found fault in the book with respect to ease of reading. They did not fault me on punctuation, spelling, or grammar; they did not fault me on lack of conciseness or clarity or making assumptions without supporting evidence; nor did they fault me on lack of cohesion in my arguments or disconnectedness in thought.

No, rather, they faulted me for having too much material to digest, not in volume of text (it was only 27 pages, including the cover) but in depth of text. Some expressed a feeling of being overwhelmed by too many terms, concepts, and historical data which they never had encountered before, or that they weren't familiar enough with the subject to track the flow of information, saying that they had to re-read previously-read material because they couldn't digest it all to remember it for later sections of the text. Still others complained of the tedium of constantly having to look up Scripture references. In fact, my wife read the first edition and commented that she had to get her Bible, a dictionary, and an encyclopedia to follow it. OK, well, I admit that I haven't found the happy medium between providing something for the masses to digest and also providing something that is defensible against the trained theologians who have vested themselves in the old, classical view on this issue, which I am challenging. For this second edition, at least I hope to minimize for the reader the tedium of endless Scripture searches by supplying key passages within the text.

A frequent comment I have received from respondents is that most readers are accustomed to reading conversational style prose as opposed to technical or business expository and persuasive styles, which are more focused on stating facts and professional opinions. A few friends stated that most people who read Christian literature assume the writer is an expert in their field and thus also assume that whatever the writer says is accurate. In other words, they felt that most readers do not want to read a deeply technical article or book and simply want the author to inform them of the big picture or major ideas without the nitty gritty details. This is problematical, because I feel the details are necessary to support a position that controverts dogma and tradition.

Nevertheless, in an effort to reach people who want the big picture without the pain of wading through the minutiae, I have provided in this summary a quick overview of the premise of this book. Here goes.

I will boldly declare herein that many of the events indicated by a correct understanding of Daniel 7 are coming true before our eyes, yet most Christians, in particular the most vocal of the prophecy teachers, preachers, and book writers, continue to maintain that the Bible does not specifically address or otherwise acknowledge the existence of the United States. There is a contingent within the bevy of prophecy proponents that believes the US is indirectly mentioned through references to geographic and geomorphic features, such as mountains and valleys that seemingly describe the US, or to "mystery Babylon" from Revelation 17:5, which these folks believe refers to pagan religions popping up in this country and our immoral and ungodly behavior being promoted throughout the globe; they also believe that descendants of the ten lost tribes of Israel form much of the population of the US.

"Mystery Babylon" and other cryptic terms in Scripture, along with nebulous and overly-vague allegories, form the basis of their position that the US will be judged harshly by God. Other prophecy proponents believe the US is not mentioned at all, even indirectly through cryptic terms, but they do believe there are spiritual parallels between the US and Israel that indicate we will be punished for our national apostasy and descent into paganism and secular humanism. Nevertheless, none of these proponents believes the US definitively can be identified through a more direct assessment of detailed prophecies in Scripture.

Daniel 7 presents a picture of un-named nations described as four beasts that function as symbols for four nations or people groups. These nations or people groups historically have been viewed by students of prophecy as ancient nations, specifically Babylon, then the combined Median and Persian empire, then the Greeks, and finally the Romans, from which the antichrist arises among the descendants of the Roman Empire. However, Daniel 7 has very noticeable traits that deviate from other Daniel prophecies regarding well-known, ancient nations; the ancient nations presented in other chapters of Daniel are identified within the text of Daniel and by our knowledge of history, but Daniel 7 has no such tools to assist the identification process.

In contrast to the ancient-nation classical view stated above, I am very confident that Scripture identifies in sufficient detail the US and other modern nations, such as Russia and the Asians. In this book, I detail the means and methods for how to identify the mysterious nations of Daniel 7. In order from first to last, they are the Anglo-American alliance, composed of the US and Great Britain, and possibly other "British-like," westernized nations like Canada and Australia; the Russians with their partners (or client states) the Turks, Syrians, and Iranians; the Asians, composed of China, India, Japan, and both Koreas, North and South; and finally the antichrist's kingdom, which engulfs the previous nations. With the exception of the antichrist's kingdom which is yet to be revealed, every one of these nations or groups of nations are the major ones currently affecting global politics and the ones routinely and prominently mentioned in the various news media. Unfortunately, Daniel 7 indicates that the US (and likely also the British) will be judged harshly and brought to a low estate, making way for the ascent of the Russians', Asians', and antichrist's kingdoms. The good news is that the US (and likely also the British) will experience national repentance and restoration of some sort before the antichrist's kingdom engulfs the whole world.

My hope is that Christians will recognize the importance of Daniel 7's prophecy, understand that we are seeing it played out now, and take action to prepare in whatever way God leads them to. I welcome those who need the details to continue on from here. I hope those tenacious enough to enter in will benefit as much from reading this book as I did from writing it.

Is The United States Mentioned In Bible Prophecy?

MAJOR POINTS

Evangelical Protestants seem to be the most vocal among the various Christian groups regarding eschatology, and in their majority view they generally hold to a pre-Tribulation rapture, millennial kingdom position. This position states that both the living and the dead members of the Body of Christ, i.e., the Church, will be caught up (raptured) to meet Christ before the Tribulation of Revelation and will return with Him at the end of the Tribulation to rule and reign on earth for 1,000 years, shortly thereafter followed by the eternal reign of Christ in the New Jerusalem.

The proponents of the majority view further state that the United States (US) is not mentioned symbolically in Bible prophecy and base their arguments on Old Testament prophecies that focus primarily on Israel and its restoration to preeminence among the nations after the return of Christ; these prophecies mention well-known nations of antiquity which are now represented by modern, descendant nations which attack Israel immediately prior to its restoration. Furthermore, they state that the New Testament does not specifically name any nations in relation to end-times interaction with Israel, other than cryptic references to Babylon in Revelation. While many prophecy scholars see parallels between the US and ancient Israel with respect to judgments they believe will befall the US as a result of its apostasy, this author has been unable to identify any significant deviations from the majority view to posit that the US is presented specifically in Scripture. One notable exception is Dr. Henry Morris in <u>The Defender's Study Bible</u>, wherein he proposes that modern nations, including the US, are represented by the four beasts of Daniel 7. This book seeks to address the weaknesses of the majority view and to provide justification that the US is presented specifically in Scripture.

Two books, Daniel and Revelation, provide the keys to answering the question regarding the US's potential involvement in Biblical prophecy. The majority view of prophecy scholars is that Daniel in particular mentions only nations of antiquity, specifically Babylon, Medo-Persia, Greece, Rome, and the revived Roman Empire, followed by the antichrist's and finally Christ's millennial kingdom. A view gaining momentum in some quarters is that Greece and Rome should be combined as one kingdom in Daniel, followed by the Muslim caliphates culminating in the Ottoman Empire, which revives to form the basis of the antichrist's kingdom. Neither of these views effectively addresses the linkage between Daniel and Revelation that helps resolve the issue of potential US involvement in Bible prophecy. Major points indicating that the US is mentioned in Bible prophecy are summarized as follows:

1. The prophecies of Daniel 2, 4, 5, 8, and 11 identify one or more nations or kingdoms (the terms "nations" and "kingdoms" are used interchangeably herein) by name, so that it is known to which nations the prophecies refer. Daniel 7 deviates from this pattern by **not** naming the nations/kingdoms that are represented by four symbolic beasts, although by deduction the antichrist's and Christ's kingdoms can

be identified in Daniel 7. This deviation hints that modern nations rather than nations of antiquity are intended.

2. The lion-eagle with plucked wings that then takes on human characteristics, the ravenous bear with three ribs, and the multi-headed leopard with wings of Daniel 7 appear to have modern equivalents by virtue of having portions of their constituent parts being presented as an amalgamated lion-bear-leopard beast in Revelation 13, which is an end-times beast. This end-times beast is the same as the "diverse" fourth beast with the teeth of iron and nails of brass in Daniel 7, an obvious reference to the kingdom of the antichrist.

3. The symbolism of Daniel 7 wherein the four winds of the compass are blowing simultaneously as the four beasts rise up from the sea (of humanity) suggests four kingdoms simultaneously vying for dominance on the world stage, but they follow one another in rapid succession. The element of rapid succession can be seen by the use of the terms "season" and "time" in Daniel 7 in reference to the duration of these kingdoms after the ascendancy of the antichrist's kingdom, where these terms indicate a few years or even months in other chapters of Daniel. In contrast, the ancient kingdoms mentioned elsewhere in Daniel were not all simultaneously vying for power, for one vanquished another in succession over hundreds of years. This contrast between the known history of the

succession of the ancient kingdoms and the picture of concurrent power struggles and succession presented in Daniel 7 further hint that modern nations rather than nations of antiquity are intended in Daniel 7.

4. Daniel 7:17 definitively indicates that the prophecy of Daniel 7, which was made during the Babylonian reign, must refer to a time beyond the times of Babylon and the other ancient kingdoms mentioned throughout Daniel, since Daniel's angelic interpreter indicated that the four beasts "**shall** arise from the earth," meaning a time **after** those ancient kingdoms. The only time in history after the times of those ancient kingdoms that shows a very strong resemblance to the prophetical four-beast vision shown in Daniel 7 is the present time, owing to the concurrent strivings of the Anglo-American alliance, the Russians with their Islamic allies, the Chinese and Asians in general, and either a revived Islamic Ottoman Empire or a revived Roman Empire through the European Union.

5. If nations of antiquity were intended to be understood as represented by the four beasts of Daniel 7, then why not use other symbols that unequivocally represent those nations elsewhere in Daniel? A ram and a goat are used to identify Medo-Persia and Greece in Daniel 8, so why not use them in Daniel 7? The fact that they were not used in Daniel 7 suggests that other nations are in mind. The beasts that are used in Daniel 7 are not used at all or, at best,

are used sparingly in artwork of the nations of antiquity, indicating that said artwork could scarcely be used as symbols to connect back to those nations for the purpose of interpreting Daniel's vision.

6. An argument from the position of logic can be made that Daniel 7 adds little value to the understanding of prophecy if it is simply a retelling of the ancient kingdoms sequence of Daniel 2's statue vision. Logic suggests that a greater value, at least for those experiencing end-times events, would be for the vision of Daniel 7 to refer to end-times nations.

7. The beasts of Daniel can be identified more readily by comparing them to symbols used for modern nations. The lion is a common symbol for Great Britain, and the eagle is **the** national symbol for the United States; the combination of the two suggests the Anglo-American alliance that has stood against tyranny together through many global conflicts. The bear is a common symbol for Russia; its ravenous, flesh-eating nature is consistent with Russian history; and modern news accounts link the three ribs in its mouth to nations with which it is currently engaging politically, specifically Islamic Iran, Syria, and Turkey. The multi-headed, multi-winged leopard can be related to Asia, since the leopard is a major motif in art and culture of Asia. China, India, Japan, and the Koreas are all prominent in geopolitical and financial issues in Asia and form the basis of the groups of four heads and four wings on the leopard beast.

8. The Anglo-American alliance is waning in power as Russia and China are waxing in power financially, politically, and militarily. Although on the surface it appears that the US is resurging as a military and financial powerhouse under President Trump, the truth is that the country is becoming more fractured, bankrupt, lawless, and hostile to the gospel. Our continued degradation is consistent with the Daniel 7 interpretation of the quick succession of the kingdoms leading up to the antichrist's kingdom. The antichrist's kingdom may have either a strong Islamic or a strong European Union flavor to it, which is also consistent with the current scenario of four powers concurrently vying against one another. Russia, with the help of its Muslim allies/clients, may exacerbate (potentially by pre-emptively attacking the US) or otherwise take advantage of the US's weakness and see this as an opportunity to attack Israel, but the prophecy of Ezekiel 38-39 (and related Psalm 83) indicates Russia's and its Islamic allies' militaries will be destroyed, leaving the Asians as the remaining super power. The destruction of the combined Russian and Islamic forces will also pave the way for a dynamic world leader to arise who will make promises of "peace and safety." Through deception he will absorb the predecessor kingdoms into his sphere of power that will be based in the kingdom of the fourth beast, ultimately plunging the world into a global conflagration leading up to the return of Christ.

9. The picture of the Anglo-American lion-eagle beast's wings being plucked shows judgment, but the picture of the lion-eagle beast being lifted up from the ground, being made to stand up like a man, and being given the heart of a man shows that *repentance and restoration* are in store for the US, the British, or both. The restoration will most certainly be spiritual, but it is less likely that political, financial, and military supremacy will be regained. The dual idea that (1) the US is mentioned in Bible prophecy and that (2) the US experiences a spiritual restoration is a major paradigm shift in current, mainline prophetical thinking.

10. The conclusion of this book is that the US is decidedly mentioned in Bible prophecy through the use of symbolism in Daniel 7 that previously has been understood incorrectly to refer to nations of antiquity. Furthermore, this paper concludes that the US will experience spiritual restoration after a time of Divine judgment.

Following the main body of this book is a discussion regarding the Ezekiel 38-39 and Psalm 83 wars. They are relevant to the main topic presented herein in that they facilitate an understanding of the succession of the kingdoms presented in Daniel 7. The major premise of the discussion of the Ezekiel 38-39 and Psalm 83 wars is that **they are pre-Tribulation wars** against Israel rather than Tribulation/Armageddon wars. The primary antagonists of these wars will be Russia and its Islamic partners. These nations will be defeated, and their defeat will set the stage for the rise of the antichrist. The primary points are numbered, typed in bold print, and supported by more detailed discussions, eliminating the need to condense the major points of the Ezekiel 38-39 and Psalm 83 wars discussion into this chapter.

IS THE UNITED STATES MENTIONED IN BIBLE PROPHECY?

Of course it is, in a general sense, since Revelation 13:7 says the antichrist is given power over all nations during the Tribulation.

And it was given unto him to make war with the saints, and to overcome them: and power was given him over all kindreds, and tongues, and nations.

Revelation 13:7

But that doesn't answer the heart of the matter on whether or not the United States (US) is mentioned specifically. In the sense that the nations of antiquity, e.g., Assyria, Egypt, Greece, and Persia, are mentioned, no, but is there some symbolism that might be used to identify the US?

Among the various groups that encompass modern Christianity, it appears to me that the most vocal group on eschatology is the evangelical Protestants, or those who emphasize: (1) the need for personal conversion; (2) sharing the gospel of Jesus Christ; (3) high regard for Biblical authority and inerrancy; and (4) proclaiming the saving death and resurrection of God the Son, Jesus Christ. Prophecy scholars within this fold generally hold to a pre-Tribulation rapture, millennial kingdom position, although there is a sizeable subculture within the evangelicals that holds to a post- or end-of-Tribulation rapture immediately before the millennial kingdom. These positions state that both the living and the dead members of the Body of Christ, i.e., the Church, will be caught up (raptured) to meet Christ before or near the end of the Tribulation of Revelation and will return with Him at the end of the Tribulation to rule and reign on earth for 1,000 years, shortly thereafter followed by the eternal reign of Christ in the New Jerusalem. As a side note to these positions, they also generally state that the US is not mentioned symbolically in Bible prophecy, with the notable exception of Dr. Henry Morris in <u>The Defender's Study Bible</u> in which he proposes that the US, Russia, and Asian nations such as China may be symbolically represented by the beasts of Daniel 7.

The majority view proponents have some strength in their argument regarding the alleged absence of the US in Scripture in that the end-times prophecies of the major and minor prophets focus primarily on Israel and its restoration to preeminence among the nations, and, for the most part, the nations that are mentioned in relation to attacks on Israel immediately prior to its restoration are those we already know about from antiquity. With reference to apocalyptic prophecy, the gospels, Acts, the end-times prophecies of the epistles of the apostles, and Revelation do not specifically name any nations besides Israel, other than somewhat cryptic references to Babylon in Revelation. However, as strong as these scholars' arguments may be, there are some significant weaknesses, and it is to these weaknesses that I want to speak.

With respect to the nations that prominently figure into prophecy, there are two books that, when linked together, describe certain nations by name and describe others through the use of symbols. These two books are Daniel and

Revelation, the two primary books that will be focused on here. A breakdown of the symbolism in each book is presented below.

Daniel 2

Spoken by Daniel to King Nebuchadnezzar regarding the king's dream:

*Thou, O king, sawest, and behold a great image. This great image, whose brightness was excellent, stood before thee; and the form thereof was terrible. *[32]* This image's head was of fine gold, his breast and his arms of silver, his belly and his thighs of brass, *[33]* His legs of iron, his feet part of iron and part of clay. *[34]* Thou sawest till that a stone was cut out without hands, which smote the image upon his feet that were of iron and clay, and brake them to pieces. *[35]* Then was the iron, the clay, the brass, the silver, and the gold, broken to pieces together, and became like the chaff of the summer threshingfloors; and the wind carried them away, that no place was found for them: and the stone that smote the image became a great mountain, and filled the whole earth.*

Daniel 2:33 - 35

This presents the statue of Nebuchadnezzar's dream. A beginning point is defined, which is the golden head of Nebuchadnezzar's Babylonian kingdom, from which it is possible to identify the other kingdoms based on our knowledge of history. Seen from the perspective of the millennialists, there are variations in the interpretation among the commentaries, but they generally agree on who the major kingdoms are: Babylon (golden head), Medo-Persia (silver chest and arms), Greece (midsection and upper legs), Rome (iron calves), and the antichrist's (mixed iron/clay feet).

Summarizing the majority view, the silver torso and arms indicate a larger kingdom yet less regal, less glorious in appearance and administrative excellence than the golden head of Babylon. The silver Medo-Persian empire had no cities equivalent to the city of Babylon and its ziggurats, massive walls, hanging gardens, and irrigation system. The brass Greeks under Alexander expanded the territory they overtook from the Medo-Persians and eventually split into four kingdoms, but in terms of Biblical, historical significance two kingdoms, the statue's thighs, were dominant, the Seleucids and the Ptolemys. The two iron legs represent the eastern and western branches of the Roman Empire, one in Rome and the other in Constantinople (modern Istanbul). The interpretations become more variable in regard to the ten toes of miry clay and iron that don't mix well. Some believe them to be the ten nations of Daniel 7:24, three of which are overthrown by the antichrist. Some commentators suggest that these may be a confederation of nations that don't mix well politically, economically, or philosophically but which, nevertheless, choose to align themselves with the antichrist during the Tribulation; many point to the European Union (EU) as the probable source of these ten nations. Some have suggested that its modern representation is the ten regions of the globe proposed by the Club of Rome, a New World Order proponent with New Age and environmentalist world views. Others claim that the global banking industry has already broken the world up into ten banking regions, although I have not researched that claim to assess its veracity. There is, however, a growing movement that revises the nation list by supplanting Rome with an Islamic kingdom, including the Ottoman Turks.

Walid Shoebat and Joel Richardson, in their book God's War on Terror: Islam, Prophecy and the Bible (see also Richardson's book The Islamic Antichrist), postulate that the antichrist's kingdom is a Muslim kingdom and that the two brass thighs are a Greco-Roman kingdom in the sense that the Romans essentially absorbed the Greeks rather than completely destroyed the Greeks by war. This would then make the two legs of iron the Muslim caliphates up until the time of the Ottoman Turks; from my own musings (and possibly others of whom I'm unaware), perhaps the two legs represent the two major branches of Islam, composed of the Sunnis and the Shias. They further propose that the ten toes of iron and miry clay (kiln-fired, hardened clay) represent intermarriage of Arabs and other peoples. The words for "mingle" and "mixed" in Daniel 2:43 (KJV) are derived from the Hebrew word "ar-ab'," such that they maintain it is a play on words that is meant to reference the Arabs and thus the Islamic peoples that form the basis of the antichrist's power. In this way they state that it is similar to Daniel's play on words for Persia in his foretelling of Belshazzar's death (see discussion below for Daniel 5), and they reject the majority view held by mainstream prophecy experts that the "revived Roman Empire" comprised of EU nations is the antichrist's kingdom based in Rome. Their argument is compelling; I do not endorse all their positions, but I wholeheartedly endorse reading their books to get a fresh perspective on prophecy.

For another perspective on the toes of the statue, in his book <u>The Redeemer's Return</u>, the great British theologian of the 20th century, A.W. Pink, posited that the miry clay mixed with the iron in the toes represents the Israelis mixing economically and philosophically with the antichrist and his kingdom during the seven year "covenant" period. Pink believed the antichrist will be Jewish. Pink's basis for the identification of the Israelis as the miry clay is the identification of Israel as clay in the Potter's hand in Isaiah 64 and Jeremiah 18. The symbolism of the clay in Daniel as a ceramic material speaks to the hardness and resistance of Israel's heart during the 3.5-year Tribulation half of the 7-year covenantal period leading up to the return of Christ, whereupon "they will look upon me (Jesus) whom they have pierced, and they shall mourn for him," and their stiff hearts will be broken. As an aside, I believe the "mourning" spoken of in Zechariah 12:10 will occur on the Day of Atonement, which is shortly thereafter followed by Tabernacles on the Jewish calendar, wherein Jesus will tabernacle among His people Israel for 1,000 years.

Another view that has gained traction in some circles is that the antichrist is Prince Charles of Wales or his son, William. They make their case based on several points, such as Charles is a literal prince; he claims to be descended from King David; he is part Greek through his father and therefore descended from one of the ancient kingdoms that will comprise part of the antichrist's kingdom; England was part of the Roman empire, thus making him of the "people of the prince who is to come"; he has embraced Islam to some extent (thus rejecting the God of his fathers); he defines himself as "the defender of faith" rather than "the defender of **the** faith (Christianity)," the moniker that his predecessors used; he claims to have had a revelatory, mystical experience in the late 1970's that redefined his mission in life; his coat of arms contains a red dragon, ten lions (heraldic beasts), and other symbols that seemingly have Biblical corollaries; and he has aligned himself with the power brokers of the EU. The proponents of this view cite numerous other points to support their case. However, my purpose for this paper is not to address the merits or lack thereof for Shoebat's, Pink's, the Charles proponents', or any other view regarding the antichrist and the fabric of his kingdom, so this issue will not be discussed further.

Daniel 4

Nebuchadnezzar has a dream in which a tree is at first glorious but then is hacked to the ground. The tree is defined as Nebuchadnezzar.

Spoken by Daniel to King Nebuchadnezzar regarding the king's dream:

The tree that thou sawest, which grew, and was strong, whose height reached unto the heaven, and the sight thereof to all the earth; [21] *Whose leaves were fair, and the fruit thereof much, and in it was meat for all; under which the beasts of the field dwelt, and upon whose branches the fowls of the heaven had their habitation:* [22] *It is thou, O king, that art grown and become strong: for thy greatness is grown, and reacheth unto heaven, and thy dominion to the end of the earth.* ²³ *And whereas the king saw a watcher and an holy one coming down from heaven, and saying, Hew the tree down, and destroy it; yet leave the stump of the roots thereof in the earth, even with a band of iron and brass, in the tender grass of the field; and let it be wet with the dew of heaven, and let his portion be with the beasts of the field, till seven times pass over him;*

Daniel 4:20-23

Daniel 5

Belshazzar the king throws a blowout party - more like a drunken orgy - but then is confronted by a hand that writes a phrase on a wall in his palace.

Then was the part of the hand sent from him; and this writing was written. ²⁵ *And this is the writing that was written, Mene, Mene, Tekel, Upharsin.* ²⁶ *This is the interpretation of the thing: Mene; God hath numbered thy kingdom, and finished it.* ²⁷ *Tekel; Thou art weighed in the balances, and art found wanting.* ²⁸ *Peres; Thy kingdom is divided, and given to the Medes and Persians.*

Daniel 5:24-28

The writing on the wall uses a plural word, Upharsin (ū·far·sin), and Daniel uses the singular version of it, Peres, in his explanation of its meaning to Belshazzar. These two words mean "split," but a double entendre is intended here in that Peres has a pronunciation similar to that for Persia. In the original Aramaic the letters are the same, differing only in the vowel points added later by the Masoretes, Jewish scribes of the first order from whom we have the text of the Old Testament. It is also interesting to note that the language spoken by the modern Persians, i.e., Iranians, is called Farsi. Daniel was telling Belshazzar that the Persians would take his kingdom, which we know from history occurred when they and their Median allies diverted the Euphrates and walked in under the gates of Babylon.

Daniel 8

Spoken by an angelic being to Daniel regarding nations of the near and far future:

And he said, Behold, I will make thee know what shall be in the last end of the indignation: for at the time appointed the end shall be. ²⁰ The ram which thou sawest having two horns are the kings of Media and Persia. ²¹ And the rough goat is the king of Grecia: and the great horn that is between his eyes is the first king. ²² Now that being broken, whereas four stood up for it, four kingdoms shall stand up out of the nation, but not in his power. ²³ And in the latter time of their kingdom, when the transgressors are come to the full, a king of fierce countenance, and understanding dark sentences, shall stand up. ²⁴ And his power shall be mighty, but not by his own power: and he shall destroy wonderfully, and shall prosper, and practise, and shall destroy the mighty and the holy people. ²⁵ And through his policy also he shall cause craft to prosper in his hand; and he shall magnify himself in his heart, and by peace shall destroy many: he shall also stand up against the Prince of princes; but he shall be broken without hand. ²⁶ And the vision of the evening and the morning which was told is true: wherefore shut thou up the vision; for it shall be for many days.

Daniel 8:19-26

The ram and the goat are defined by the angel as Medo-Persia, then Greece. The one larger horn of the ram is the Persian part, which came to be the more dominant partner of the alliance. The great horn of the goat was Alexander, whose kingdom was broken into four lesser horns under his four generals: Ptolemy to the south (Egypt and north Africa, one brass thigh of Daniel 2, according to the majority view), Seleucus to the east (Israel, Syria, and Lebanon, the other brass thigh of Daniel 2, according to the majority view), Lysimachus to the north, and Cassander to the west. The little horn is none other than the antichrist. The intrigues of the Ptolemys and Seleucids are chronicled in Daniel 11.

Daniel 11

The beginning point is defined as the four kings after Cyrus, being Cambyses, Smerdis, Darius Hystaspes, and Xerxes, which then allows us to piece together the other kingdoms in order based on our knowledge of history. A full citation of Daniel 11 is too lengthy for our purposes, but select passages are presented below to show the major players.

Spoken by an angelic being to Daniel regarding Daniel's vision from the preceding chapter 10:

Also I in the first year of Darius the Mede, even I, stood to confirm and to strengthen him. ²And now will I shew thee the truth. Behold, there shall stand up yet three kings in Persia [Cambyses, Smerdis, Darius Hystaspes]; *and the fourth* [Xerxes] *shall be far richer than they all: and by his strength through his riches he shall stir up all against the realm of Grecia.*

³ And a mighty king [Alexander] shall stand up, that shall rule with great dominion, and do according to his will. ⁴ And when he shall stand up, his kingdom shall be broken, and shall be divided toward the four winds [Ptolemy, Seleucus, Lysimachus, and Cassander] of heaven; and not to his posterity, nor according to his dominion which he ruled: for his kingdom shall be plucked up, even for others beside those....

Daniel 11:1-4; 25-37

Several centuries of war between the Seleucids and the Ptolemys bring us to Antiochus Epiphanes, a Seleucid, who attacks the Ptolemaic king, Ptolemy VI Philometor, in Egypt.

²⁵ And he shall stir up his power and his courage against the king of the south with a great army; and the king of the south shall be stirred up to battle with a very great and mighty army; but he shall not stand: for they shall forecast devices against him. ²⁶ Yea, they that feed of the portion of his meat shall destroy him, and his army shall overflow: and many shall fall down slain. ²⁷ And both of these kings' hearts shall be to do mischief, and they shall speak lies at one table; but it shall not prosper: for yet the end shall be at the time appointed. ²⁸ Then shall he return into his land with great riches; and his heart shall be against the holy covenant; and he shall do exploits, and return to his own land. ²⁹ At the time appointed he shall return, and come toward the south; but it shall not be as the former, or as the latter. ³⁰ For the ships of Chittim shall come against him: therefore he shall be grieved, and return, and have indignation against the holy covenant: so shall he do; he shall even return, and have intelligence with them that forsake the holy covenant. ³¹ And arms shall stand on his part, and they shall pollute the sanctuary of strength, and shall take away the daily sacrifice, and they shall place the abomination that maketh desolate. [The Jewish historian, Flavius Josephus, records in <u>Antiquities of the Jews,</u> Book XII, Chapter 5 that Antiochus Epiphanes sacrificed a pig on the altar in the temple. Coins Antiochus minted during his reign have his profile and are inscribed with the epithet "theos epiphanes", or "manifest god." In this manner, he is a type or foreshadowing of the antichrist.] *[32] And such as do wickedly against the covenant shall he corrupt by flatteries: but the people that do know their God* [the Maccabees, Jews who led a revolt against Antiochus Epiphanes] *shall be strong, and do exploits.*

A transition from the time of the Maccabees to periods much later in Jewish history occurs at verse 33.

...[33] And they that understand among the people shall instruct many: yet they shall fall by the sword, and by flame, by captivity, and by spoil, many days. [34] Now when they shall fall, they shall be holpen with a little help: but many shall cleave to them with flatteries. [35] And some of them of understanding shall fall, to try them, and to purge, and to make them white, even to the time of the end: because it is yet for a time appointed. [These three verses mark a transition from the history of the Seleucids and Ptolemys to the history of the Jews from the time of the diaspora after the Romans destroyed Jerusalem in 70 A.D. until the time of the antichrist.]

Finally, the antichrist is presented.

...[36] And the king [antichrist] *shall do according to his will; and he shall exalt himself, and magnify himself above every god, and shall speak marvellous things against the God of gods, and shall prosper till the indignation be accomplished: for that that is*

determined shall be done. ³⁷ Neither shall he regard the God of his fathers, nor the desire of women, nor regard any god: for he shall magnify himself above all.

For those in the reading audience who want to explore all of Daniel 11, the players that are discussed therein are predominantly the Ptolemys and the Seleucids, although the Romans are also mentioned as "ships from Chittim," or Cyprus, in verse 30. The antichrist is discussed in verses 36 to 45. Some may wonder why the Romans are associated with Cyprus, since many consider it in classical times as more aligned with the Greeks; its name is derived from a Greek word for copper, *kupros*, and the predominant language and culture in modern times is Greek. The "ships of Chittim" in Daniel 11:30 are the Macedonian-Greek, or possibly Italian, vessels in which the Roman ambassador Popillius Laenas arrived to warn the Seleucid king Antiochus Epiphanes (a pre-type of the antichrist) not to attack the Ptolemaic city, Alexandria. As Kedar generally represents the East, in like manner Chittim represents the West (Jeremiah 2:10), including Rome. The point of this discussion is to demonstrate that we know who the nations were so as to provide a contrast to Daniel 7.

Daniel 7

We have now arrived at the crux of the issue. I have placed this chapter out of order in the discussion because an understanding of the other Daniel chapters helps in the understanding of this chapter in relation to our topic. This chapter is so critical to our discussion that I feel compelled to quote all of it.

In the first year of Belshazzar king of Babylon Daniel had a dream and visions of his head upon his bed: then he wrote the dream, and told the sum of the matters. ² Daniel spake and said, I saw in my vision by night, and, behold, the four winds of the heaven strove upon the great sea. ³ And four great beasts came up from the sea, diverse one from another. ⁴ The first was like a lion, and had eagle's wings: I beheld till the wings thereof were plucked, and it was lifted up from the earth, and made stand upon the feet as a man, and a man's heart was given to it. ⁵ And behold another beast, a second, like to a bear, and it raised up itself on one side, and it had three ribs in the mouth of it between the teeth of it: and they said thus unto it, Arise, devour much flesh. ⁶ After this I beheld, and lo another, like a leopard, which had upon the back of it four wings of a fowl; the beast had also four heads; and dominion was given to it. ⁷ After this I saw in the night visions, and behold a fourth beast, dreadful and terrible, and strong exceedingly; and it had great iron teeth: it devoured and brake in pieces, and stamped the residue with the feet of it: and it was diverse from all the beasts that were before it; and it had ten horns. ⁸ I considered the horns, and, behold, there came up among them another little horn, before whom there were three of the first horns plucked up by the roots: and, behold, in this horn were eyes like the eyes of man, and a mouth speaking great things. ⁹ I beheld till the thrones were cast down, and the Ancient of days did sit, whose garment was white as snow, and the hair of his head like the pure wool: his throne was like the fiery flame, and his wheels as burning fire. ¹⁰ A fiery stream issued and came forth from before him: thousand thousands ministered unto him, and ten thousand times ten thousand stood before him: the judgment was set, and the books were opened. ¹¹ I beheld then because of the voice of the great words which the horn

Paul R. Wild

spake: I beheld even till the beast was slain, and his body destroyed, and given to the burning flame. [12] *As concerning the rest of the beasts, they had their dominion taken away: yet their lives were prolonged for a season and time.* [13] *I saw in the night visions, and, behold, one like the Son of man came with the clouds of heaven, and came to the Ancient of days, and they brought him near before him.* [14] *And there was given him dominion, and glory, and a kingdom, that all people, nations, and languages, should serve him: his dominion is an everlasting dominion, which shall not pass away, and his kingdom that which shall not be destroyed.* [15] *I Daniel was grieved in my spirit in the midst of my body, and the visions of my head troubled me.* [16] *I came near unto one of them that stood by, and asked him the truth of all this. So he told me, and made me know the interpretation of the things.* [17] *These great beasts, which are four, are four kings, which shall arise out of the earth.* [18] *But the saints of the most High shall take the kingdom, and possess the kingdom for ever, even for ever and ever.* [19] *Then I would know the truth of the fourth beast, which was diverse from all the others, exceeding dreadful, whose teeth were of iron, and his nails of brass; which devoured, brake in pieces, and stamped the residue with his feet;* [20] *And of the ten horns that were in his head, and of the other which came up, and before whom three fell; even of that horn that had eyes, and a mouth that spake very great things, whose look was more stout than his fellows.* [21] *I beheld, and the same horn made war with the saints, and prevailed against them;* [22] *Until the Ancient of days came, and judgment was given to the saints of the most High; and the time came that the saints possessed the kingdom.* [23] *Thus he said, The fourth beast shall be the fourth kingdom upon earth, which shall be diverse from all kingdoms, and shall devour the whole earth, and shall tread it down, and break it in pieces. ²⁴ And the ten horns out of this kingdom are ten kings that shall arise: and another shall rise after them; and he shall be diverse from the first, and he shall subdue three kings. ²⁵ And he shall speak great words against the most High, and shall wear out the saints of the most High, and think to change times and laws: and they shall be given into his hand until a time and times and the dividing of time. ²⁶ But the judgment shall sit, and they shall take away his dominion, to consume and to destroy it unto the end. ²⁷ And the kingdom and dominion, and the greatness of the kingdom under the whole heaven, shall be given to the people of the saints of the most High, whose kingdom is an everlasting kingdom, and all dominions shall serve and obey him. ²⁸ Hitherto is the end of the matter. As for me Daniel, my cogitations much troubled me, and my countenance changed in me: but I kept the matter in my heart.*

Daniel 7

The vision begins with the winds from all four directions striving against one another, alluding to four kingdoms that exist simultaneously, competing against one another for supremacy, and inhabiting the four points of the compass in relation to one another. Verse 3 indicates that four beasts rise up from the maelstrom of the sea and wind, again suggesting concurrent kingdoms rising up from the sea of humanity. But there is no identification by the angelic being speaking to Daniel of whom these beasts represent. **In this way, Daniel 7 deviates from the pattern of the other chapters in that *none* of the four symbols is defined.** Although the kingdoms are concurrent, verse 4 suggests an element of sequence in that "first" the lion with eagle's wings is presented. It is not clear if the "first" means it is only the first to be considered by Daniel without reference to succession of kingdoms in the way the other chapters of Daniel present successive kingdoms, or if it is the first kingdom that God intends to judge and then remove from power. I believe it to be the latter in that, even though the kingdoms are initially vying for power simultaneously, the kingdoms will wane in power in quick succession until the final kingdom of Christ is established.

The four beasts are in succession a lion with eagle's wings that then is given a heart and made to stand upright like a man; a ravenous, flesh-eating bear with three ribs in its mouth and weighted to one side; a leopard with four wings and four heads; and finally an undescribed beast with the exception of iron teeth, brass nails, some horns, and a loud mouth. It is left up to us to deduce who they are.

If we start from the back and work forward, the fourth beast, according to the majority view, appears to represent the Roman Empire, from which the antichrist springs to subdue three of ten kingdoms in what is called by many scholars "the revived Roman Empire." The majority view among the commentaries is that the other beasts represent from the Romans in reverse order Greece, Medo-Persia, and Babylon. Some commentators believe that the beast that is made to stand upright like a man and given the heart of a man is Nebuchadnezzar of Babylon in that he ultimately did repent and express faith in the One True God and thus became (presumably) a benevolent king. The problem with the majority view is that it ignores the book of Revelation and its linkage to Daniel.

Daniel and Revelation provide the keys to unlock each other, such that it is difficult if not impossible to fully understand one without the other. In most instances, Daniel provides symbolism and terminology that unlock Revelation, but it can work in reverse. One such instance is Revelation 13. In this passage a beast that is part lion, part leopard, and part bear is described and is placed within the timeframe of the 3.5 years before the return of Christ. It would seem reasonable that there would be a corresponding passage in Daniel that also describes this beast. As it turns out, there is, as we saw in our previous discussion of Daniel 7.

Now that we've established a linkage between Daniel 7 and Revelation 13, are there any indications of the timing of these kingdoms? Well, as stated earlier, the amalgamated lion-bear-leopard beast of Revelation 13 is placed within the 3.5-year Tribulation period leading up to the return of Christ, so is there any corresponding indication in Daniel? A clue in Daniel 7:12 suggests that the three kingdoms described by the lion-eagle, the bear, and the winged leopard will be in quick succession before the final, fourth, worldwide kingdom from which the antichrist springs. It says that the people of these three kingdoms have their lives prolonged for a season and a time, which some might argue could also be applied to the ancient kingdoms of Babylon, Medo-Persia, and Greece in that remnants of these people groups were absorbed by each successive kingdom and still exist two to two and one-half millennia later. However, the uses of the terms "season" and "time" suggest years and months rather than millennia because of the uses of these terms elsewhere in Scripture where they refer to time spans of a few years and probably include the idea of months. The Hebrew root word for "season" is "zevan" and is used 11 times in Scripture in the context of limited periods, certainly not centuries or millennia, including Daniel 4:36 where it refers to the seven-year period Nebuchadnezzar went insane. Daniel 4:23,25 use the word "times" – Hebrew "iddan" - in reference to Nebuchadnezzar's period of insanity, so it cannot refer to millennia. It cannot refer to even as long a period as a decade, since we know from Daniel 9:25-27 one "week" of years, or seven years, is the longest that the antichrist can hope to have any influence. "Time" is used in Daniel 12:7 to refer to a year. Thus, from our findings on the uses of words to define time in Daniel, we can conclude that the three beasts of Daniel 7:12 immediately precede the antichrist's kingdom and have modern rather than historical representation.

But there is a more decisive and stronger point that lays the majority view to rest, the proverbial "final nail in the coffin." Daniel 7:17 places Daniel's vision in the future, for it says these are four beasts "which **shall** arise from the earth," making it certain that the vision could not begin with Babylon and was intended to indicate a future event. The Babylonian king, Belshazzar, was in power at the time of the vision, but the Medo-Persians were a major, competing power at the same time and ultimately overtook the Babylonians, so the vision's fulfillment would necessarily have to begin at some point **after** the Babylonians and Medo-Persians. This, then, also would preclude the Greeks and Romans from consideration because the first two kingdoms could not be considered, thereby upsetting the majority view of the identification of the kingdoms.

As a final point (albeit, I admit, a somewhat subjective point) to bolster my position that Daniel 7 is an end-times prophecy, I would ask how the majority view adds value to the understanding of future events if it is simply another version of the statue vision of Daniel 2? Wasn't one vision enough to show the order of ancient kingdoms from the time of Nebuchadnezzar to the antichrist's kingdom?

The First Beast – The Anglo-American Lion with Eagle's Wings

Now, since I have taken the position that Daniel's vision in chapter 7 relates to modern times, the next step is to deduce who these modern equivalents may be. Let us first examine the descriptions of the beasts of Daniel 7 themselves. The first is described as part eagle and part lion. To me, the only modern kingdom that this could describe is the Anglo-American alliance, the beast of the western wind. The alliance of England and its former colonies (e.g., Canada and Australia) with the United States has successfully defended the world from tyrants through two world wars and is currently doing so against Islamic terrorists. The lion is the larger part, indicating the larger geographic reach and longer duration of the British portion of the beast relative to the smaller American eagle portion of it. The lion is a dominant theme in British art and heraldry, even forming a part of the crest of the royal house of Windsor, and we very well know the significance of the eagle in the American psyche.

There may be some in the reading audience who will protest, "But the Babylonians used winged lions in their artwork, and wasn't Nebuchadnezzar likened to a lion and an eagle somewhere in the Bible?" OK, so, let's dig into this.

Ancient Mesopotamian art includes winged lions, winged bulls, or simple lions and bulls. Many people associate winged lions with Babylon, but it was the Assyrians who used this visual art motif. This motif can be seen in the Assyrian lamassu, sculpted creatures that were winged lions or winged bulls. Variants of the lamassu can be seen in the Persians' griffins, mythical creatures that were winged lions with horns, in their artwork at their capital of Susa. In contrast, the Babylonians used unwinged lions and bulls; these can be seen on cylinder seals uncovered from Babylonian excavations. The cylinder seals, or picture stories, were used to emboss images onto two-dimensional surfaces, like cloth or clay tablets. Unwinged lions were placed in the bricks used to build the Processional Way of the city of Babylon, and unwinged dragons and bulls were placed on the Ishtar Gate of the city. This is not an exhaustive study to say that the winged lion was never used in Babylonian art or symbology but rather to say that, if it ever was used, it was not a dominant theme that immediately links that symbol to the kingdom of Babylon. As for Nebuchadnezzar, it is true that he was likened to a lion by Jeremiah (Jeremiah 4:7) and an eagle by Ezekiel (Ezekiel 17:3), but again, the placement of fulfillment of the vision in the future (Daniel 7:17) definitively precludes Nebuchadnezzar from being considered.

The Second Beast – The Russian Bear with Turkish, Syrian, and Iranian Ribs

I believe the second beast of Daniel 7, the ravenous, flesh-eating bear, represents Russia of the northern wind. It should not be equated with the Medo-Persian kingdom, which is defined elsewhere as a ram in Daniel 8. To my knowledge, the bear is not used in Persian art of antiquity, but rather predominantly the bull and the lion, and to a lesser extent the horse, lynx, and ungulates (deer or antelope like creatures) of various types. Back in the 1980's, Ronald Reagan used a political TV ad to communicate to the American people the need to rebuild our military to stand up to the aggression of the Russians. To do this, Reagan used a bear as a symbol for the Russians. This motif has been used extensively in political cartoons for decades now and has made the bear synonymous with Russia throughout the world. The ravenous nature of Daniel's bear is certainly consistent with the history of the Russian tsars and the Marxists in that they both thought nothing of eating the flesh (the health and wealth) of their own people. Nor did they give a second thought to devouring the Warsaw Pact nations behind the Iron Curtain or the neighboring states of Georgia, Latvia, Lithuania, Estonia, and the "stan" republics. The current Putin regime isn't much better, as their invasion of Ukraine further reveals, and will, according to my interpretation of Ezekiel 38, attempt to devour Israel in collusion with its Islamic allies.

Paul R. Wild

Daniel also saw the bear weighted to or raised up on one side, possibly alluding to the dominance of the Slavic ethnicity of Russia over other ethnicities, or perhaps this weightedness alludes to the ethnographic division of the country wherein the western portion of the country has a more European (and more dominant) complexion, and the eastern portion has a more Asiatic complexion. Maybe it refers to the dominant religious culture of Christianity (the Orthodox Church was the major religio-cultural influence until the rise of the Marxists) versus lesser religious cultures, such as Islam; or perhaps the converse is true in that Russia is tipping its political and military might toward external Islamic regimes and away from its historical Christian base. As for the three ribs in its mouth, Henry Morris suggested these are nations that abut Russia and which have been dominated, overshadowed, or manipulated by Russia throughout their own history. Morris postulated that the Baltic states of Latvia, Lithuania, and Estonia are the three ribs, but I believe there are much better candidates that can be identified by simply watching the news.

A November 5, 2007 online article by the Fars News Agency of Tehran (Fars is a province in Iran and is derived from the ancient name the Persians called their homeland, Parsa, which is retained in the term "Pars" or "Fars," from which the name of their language, "Farsi," is derived) had the headline, "Inevitable Iran-Turkey-Syria-Russia Alliance" and ended with, "The final effect of the region's aversion to American policies will be the formation of the "union of four:" Russia, Turkey, Iran and Syria. Of course, this rapprochement between Ankara, Moscow, Damascus and

Tehran will definitely affect Washington's position in the Middle East." Without them knowing the prophetical implications, it appears that the Iranians have identified for us the three ribs in the bear's mouth. I began the first edition of this book in 2009 and completed it in 2011. Since 2011, all four of these nations have become prominent in global news and are among the major players in Middle Eastern politics.

The suggestion that Russia is mentioned in Daniel through the use of symbols is supported elsewhere in Scripture. Consider the following:

And the word of the Lord came unto me, saying, ² Son of man, set thy face against Gog, the land of Magog, the chief prince of Meshech and Tubal, and prophesy against him, ³ And say, Thus saith the Lord God; Behold, I am against thee, O Gog, the chief prince of Meshech and Tubal: ⁴ And I will turn thee back, and put hooks into thy jaws, and I will bring thee forth, and all thine army, horses and horsemen, all of them clothed with all sorts of armour, even a great company with bucklers and shields, all of them handling swords: ⁵ Persia, Ethiopia, and Libya with them; all of them with shield and helmet: ⁶ Gomer, and all his bands; the house of Togarmah of the north quarters, and all his bands: and many people with thee.

Ezekiel 38:1-6

Ezekiel 38:2 in the King James Bible, as quoted above, uses the term "chief prince," whereas the New American Standard Bible uses the term Rosh. Both are reasonable interpretations, since Rosh means head or chief prince and is transliterated in the NASB from the Hebrew as a formal name rather than as its translated meaning in the KJV, "chief prince." There are very learned scholars on both sides that disagree, with reasonable arguments for their respective positions on whether to translate Rosh as a proper name or as its meaning, "chief prince." My opinion is that "chief prince" is the preferred translation, as it is shown in the KJV.

Now, if one were inclined to go with Rosh, it brings to mind the similar sounding Russia. Meshech and Tubal are considered by many scholars to have as their modern equivalents Moscow and Tobolsk. If you were to draw a line on a map of Russia between Moscow to the west and Tobolsk to the east, you would be drawing a line between the approximate western and eastern boundaries of historical White Russia, i.e., the distinctly Russian (Slavic) people that migrated north of the Caucasus Mountains and from whence came the term Caucasian. Furthermore, Ezekiel 38:6,15 indicate that Rosh's invading army will come from the north "quarters" or "parts." The nations aligning with Rosh will be nations that Russia is currently courting, i.e., the Muslim nations surrounding Israel. These nations buy Russian armaments and have received training and support from the Russian military. For further discussion on the war of Ezekiel 38, see the chapter on Ezekiel 38 at the rear of the book.

For an alternate view, Shoebat, Richardson, and an increasing number of students of prophecy believe that the references to Meshech and Tubal are references to the regions of Turkey rather than Russia, specifically the *Moschki/Mushki* and *Tubalu/Tibareni* peoples that inhabited ancient Anatolia (modern Turkey). The basis of their position would take too much time and space to elaborate on here, but suffice it to say that they make a strong case that Turkey is a major player in Ezekiel's vision of the invading hordes. Richardson has an entire web page dedicated to proving that Russia is not the Gog, Magog, or Togarmah of Ezekiel 38 and makes a seemingly strong argument for Turkey as the leader of the invading armies. He goes to great lengths to discount the arguments of others who use the writings of ancient historians to make their case that Magog is Russia, saying that some of these ancient sources don't actually support the concept that Magog is Russia. See the following:

http://www.propheticalschool.com/interpreting-gog-magog-invasion-joel-richardson/

But I disagree with him. It is possible to examine some of these ancient sources and link them together to get a picture of who the Magogites' descendants are. We will examine three ancient sources: Herodotus, the Greek world traveler and historian who lived in the 5th century B.C.; Josephus, the 1st century A.D. Jewish historian; and Claudius Ptolemy, the Greco-Egyptian writer and mathematician of the 2nd century A.D. We will begin with Herodotus, who introduces us to the Scythians.

Herodotus, Book IV: 20

Callippidae on the north coast of the Black Sea, beyond [which] is a mixed race part Scythian and part Greek; beyond them is a people named Alazones. Both these follow the Scythian way of life. Beyond these are Scythians who till and sow, not for food, but for sale. Beyond them are the Neuri and to the northward of those the land is uninhabited as far as we know.

Ptolemy expands our understanding of the Scythians.

Ptolemy, Book 2, Chapter 2: Of the Characteristics of the Inhabitants of the General Climes

*Those who live under the more northern parallels, those, I mean, who have the **Bears** [Please note the reference to bears, i.e., Ursa Major/Ursa Minor, Big Dipper/Little Dipper.] over their heads, since they are far removed from the zodiac and the heat of the sun, are therefore cooled; but because they have a richer share of moisture, which is most nourishing and is not there exhausted by heat, they are white in complexion, straight-haired, tall and well-nourished, and somewhat cold by nature; these too are savage in their habits because their dwelling-places are continually cold. The wintry character of their climate, the size of their plants, and the wildness of their animals are in accord with these qualities. We call these men, too, by a general name, Scythians.*

Josephus connects the dots for us.

Flavius Josephus, Antiquities of the Jews, Book 1, Chapter 6:1

Magog founded those that from him were named Magogites, but who are by the Greeks called Scythians.

Therefore, the Scythians were descendants of Magog who lived in cold, northern climates - certainly north of the Black Sea, which itself is to the north of modern Turkey -

and had fair skin and straight hair. Sounds like Russians to me.

There is too much other information from other ancient sources, such as Strabo, Tacitus, Homer, Procopius, Jordanes, Arrian, and even Darius the Great, who recorded his defeat of the Scythians on the Behistun Rock located in modern Iran, that can be pieced together to demonstrate that the Scythians were a northern people in addition to their presence in what is now modern Turkey. It is interesting to note Ptolemy's reference to bears in his discussion of the Scythians, something that I do not think is coincidental and certainly brings to mind the Russian bear.

Let's further consider Ezekiel 38:6,15 in which "north quarters/parts" are presented. Why is this important? The term "north quarters" provides us a geographic reference that is more clear than trying to establish geographic boundaries using the titular heads of nations mentioned in Ezekiel 38, since there is not complete agreement among historians regarding the geographic boundaries of those ancient nations. The term "north quarters" is a translation of the Hebrew root word "yerekah." Translations of this word from various Bible versions include remote, side, rear, flank, extreme parts, recesses, border, coast, quarters, uttermost, *ad nauseum*. Even Jerome, the translator of the Hebrew Bible into the Latin Vulgate used by the Roman Catholics, translated yerekah as latera, further translated as "parts" in English; latera is from the Latin root latus for lateral in English, which we know as "side." Lexicons and concordances, such as Brown Driver Briggs, Strong's, and

Hendrickson's Interlinear, are in agreement with respect to the translation of yerekah as an extreme location.

I have a tendency to go with the KJV where translations vary because I feel the KJV translators understood the underlying theology better than other translators. So, let's take the KJV's take on it and explore "quarters" from verse 6. If quarters are 45 degree sections north pole to south pole, then latitude 45 degrees north of the equator would include Russia, not Turkey. If we take anything north of the equator and apply quartering to those regions, then quarters would be 22.5 degrees and place the northernmost quarter at latitude 67.5 degrees north, definitely in Russia and most definitely not in Turkey.

My final point to offer for making the case that Gog and Magog are Russia is that ignoring Russia and supplanting it with Turkey is akin to ignoring the 900-lb gorilla in the room. Russia dwarfs Turkey in every meaningful way imaginable, from sheer geographic size to military might to global influence to population to wealth to natural resources to aggression. Russia moved into Ukraine, but Turkey did not; Russia moved into Syria, but Turkey did not. (Although, as of the time of completing this book, Turkey has bombed US allies in Syria and is amassing troops along the Turkey-Syria border wall it is building.) If anything, the Russians surely are showing a tendency to move south. Next stop, perhaps Israel?

In conclusion, taking a hard position that Russia cannot be included as a modern counterpart to Gog and Magog is not tenable. Because of the nomadic nature of the

Magogites, it is very likely that their descendants are represented in both modern Turkey and Russia. Thus, my opinion is that both Russia and its Islamic allies (or perhaps vassals is a better term), including Turkey, are in view as the invading armies of Ezekiel 38, with Russia as the leader. In the very least, that opinion is certainly supported by the relatively current Iranian news, as presented above, and by current events.

The Third Beast – The Four-Winged, Four-Headed Asian Leopard

I believe the third beast of Daniel 7, the four-winged, four-headed leopard, represents Asia of the eastern wind. The majority view among classical commentaries is that it is Greece, but the leopard has only a token place in Greek art of antiquity as, for example, can be seen with the leopards that the Greek god Dionysus rode, and his leopards were not winged or multi-headed. What I have found in my research on this issue is that when the leopard was used in Greek art, it post-dated the times of Alexander and his four generals. In any case, the leopard is not a major motif in Greek art or symbology. If the Greeks were intended, then why not use the goat symbol that was used for Greece in Daniel 8? The same could be said for the bear – if the Medo-Persians were intended rather than the Russians, then why not use the ram symbol of Daniel 8?

The historical, territorial range of the leopard has been predominantly Asia (and also Africa), not Europe (some commentators believe the leopard represents France or Germany). The leopard is a dominant theme in art and literature in Asia, and the Chinese even developed a kung fu style named after it. The leopard, *Panthera pardis*, possesses yellow fur (notwithstanding the white snow leopard, *Panthera uncia*, a rare and highly isolated species) with many black spots, suggesting the "yellow" skin of many Asian peoples. The four wings and four heads suggest four distinct nations or people groups. I believe these are modern China, India, Japan, and the Koreas, all of which are currently the most prominent among Asian nations in terms of worldwide news coverage and political, military, and economic influence. Perhaps one of the heads could represent all the other nations of Indochina rather than the Koreas, but I'm betting that both North and South Korea comprise one head, based on current events.

Is The United States Mentioned In Bible Prophecy?

Current Events

During the time of Daniel, he recognized the prophecies of Jeremiah were about to come true in relation to Israel being reestablished in its land. He had a more precise understanding of the coming events of that general timeframe than we do now for our timeframe since he knew 70 years were to pass since the time of Nebuchadnezzar before the Israelites were to begin the process of returning to Israel. He read the signs of the times in light of prophecy to understand what the near-future held. I believe we can do the same, since Scripture supports this. The angel of Daniel 12 told Daniel that man's knowledge would increase, from which we can deduce that our knowledge of prophecy will also increase. That being said, it seems reasonable to observe what is going on in the world to see if there are any patterns or circumstances that have a Biblical corollary.

OK, so, what is going on in the world? We see three super powers, the US, Russia, and China, flexing their military and economic muscles. One of these, the US, along with its Anglo ally, England, is on the wane both militarily and economically. (I would caution against irrational exuberance over Trump's recent economic and military victories; we are still $20 trillion in debt and growing, with massive upgrades needed to our defense forces.)

More so than in the previous 30+ years since the Reagan military build-up, the US/British Anglo-American alliance can now be seriously challenged militarily by both Russia and China, and as our nation is sliding toward a massive depression, Russia has taken its oil cash from the last five years to build up its military, and the Chinese have taken over our manufacturing sector. An article in online *Investopedia*, dated August 6, 2015, stated that, as of January 2015, China and Japan both own about one and a quarter trillion dollars of US Treasury bills. China has become more vocal about its doubts regarding buying any more T bills because of worries the US can't pay on them. Russia has reintroduced military movements in areas close to or in US air space, sea, and land, and it has conducted joint military exercises with China in recent years.

Here is what I said in 2011:

Turning our attention to the US itself, the leadership of our federal government has refused to press charges against Black Panthers who were intimidating white voters at polls in Pennsylvania; has stated it will refuse to enforce the Defense of Marriage Act; has repealed the "don't ask-don't tell" policy in the military, even though the majority of the military does not want openly homosexual people serving in the military; and has advanced a budget that is projected to have a $1.6 trillion deficit for fiscal year 2011, further aggravating the $14+ trillion we are already in debt, even as it debates raising the debt cap. A Fox News online article of April 19, 2011, read "Top credit rating service demotes U.S. fiscal outlook from a 'stable' to 'negative' as politicians reaffirm their commitment to solving the debt crisis."

Our government refuses to acknowledge federal courts that have declared the healthcare bill as unconstitutional, as well as ignoring the numerous State and private lawsuits challenging the bill. In addition to the wars in Afghanistan and Iraq, we are fighting a third war along our Mexican border with illegal aliens and drug lords; we are losing that war. We have a federal government that increasingly ignores the rule of law for its own ends and has all the appearances of completely marginalizing the Constitution. We are but a hairsbreadth away from totalitarianism.

As dangerous as these things are to the health of our nation, nothing compares to the deadly tact Obama has taken by calling for Israel to return to its pre-1967 borders, since it effectively calls for Israel to commit suicide and empowers Israel's Muslim enemies to commit genocide. Any nation who curses Israel curses itself (Genesis 12:2-3). There are some Christians who say that a mere taste of the coming judgment was the tornadoes and severe weather which struck numerous locations in the US in the few days following Obama's May 19, 2011 speech. Some have done extensive research to document what they believe is a clear pattern in the last 20 years of American policy makers snubbing Israel followed immediately by domestic economic and natural disasters that seemingly indicate Divine chastisement. This idea is beyond the extent of this paper, but it is certainly food for thought.

As for Russia, Fox reported on April 20, 2011, that Russia currently pumps more oil than Saudi Arabia, holds almost $500 billion in currency reserves, has the world's seventh largest economy, and has recently launched a $700 billion drive to modernize its nuclear and conventional military forces by 2020. Russian Prime Minister Putin has boasted that Russia has an economic growth rate of 4% and expects to fully recover from the current global financial crisis by 2012. Russia expands while the US contracts and sinks further into moral depravity and apostasy.

Regarding Russia's allies, Ahmadinejad of Iran has stated publicly and privately that he believes the return of the Islamic 12th Imam, or Mahdi, their Islamic messiah, is imminent and that Muslims must hasten the return of the Mahdi by destroying Israel. In general, Islamists such as Hezbollah and the Muslim Brotherhood believe that the reason the Muslims have not been able to defeat Israel in the wars between the Arab states and Israel since 1948 is that the Arab states have not been ruled by Islamic theocracies and, therefore, their Allah has not blessed them in order to defeat Israel.

While ignorant Americans applaud the advance of "democracy" in the Middle East through the revolutions in Tunisia, Egypt, and Libya, and the other revolutions brewing in Syria, Bahrain, Yemen, and Jordan, the truth is that worse regimes will result. Democracy can be used to "democratically" elect by the majority a violent Islamic regime if the majority of voters are Muslims. This is what happened when Reza Pahlavi of Iran was deposed in 1979 and Khomeini and his Islamic regime took over. Even now in Egypt and Iraq where the strongmen of the Middle East, such as Mubarak and Hussein, have been removed from power, the increase in violence against Christians by Muslims has gone exponential. Shoebat believes a transnational Islamic regime will comprise the larger part of the fourth beast; he makes a strong if not completely convincing case for this. In any case, as I observe American Christians foolishly rooting for "democratic reform" in these countries, I can think only of Hosea 4:6 – "My people are destroyed for lack of knowledge…"

Finally, the Chinese recently have introduced their own stealth bomber and a new missile system; have called for the removal of the US dollar as the global currency standard, as have the French and others; and have rebuffed our president's calls for more open trade and ceasing of the Chinese government's artificial maintenance of the yuan at artificially weak levels, giving China an unfair trade advantage. The Chinese rebuff to Obama was perceived in the global community as a slap in our face and a victory for the Chinese. Adding fuel to the fire, the headline for Fox News online for April 25, 2011, read "IMF Predicts Chinese Economy to Surpass U.S. in 2016."

It is not far-fetched to suggest that we will see a rapid succession of the Anglo-American alliance, Russia and its Islamic allies, and the Chinese/Asian hordes leading up to the kingdom from which the antichrist will come. Whether he comes from a revived Roman kingdom of the majority view or an Islamic kingdom of Shoebat's view, this kingdom of the southern wind (relative to the northern Russia) will absorb or comprise parts of these kingdoms. Could it be that the US will fall through economic chaos and possible surprise nuclear attacks from one of the other super powers, thus allowing Russia to feel emboldened to invade Israel with its Muslim allies, only to be destroyed? Many times in Biblical history God punished His people using a more wicked nation, then judged that wicked nation, finally calling His people back to repentance and restoration. This method caused the prophet Habakkuk much distress, but it also may elicit in US the same thing that it did for Habakkuk: "But the just shall live by his faith." I believe this point suggests that Russia will be used by God as a rod of correction for US. Nevertheless, when Russia and the Muslim hordes do invade Israel, Ezekiel 38 and 39 and the parallel passage of Psalm 83 make it very clear that they will be destroyed. With two super powers and the Muslims largely out of the way, only the Asians are left as a major power, powerful enough to field a 200 million-man army (Revelation 9:16). But the fall of the Anglo-American alliance and Russia with its Muslim allies would also pave the way for a dynamic world leader to make an agreement with Israel and make promises of "peace and safety" (1 Thessalonians 5:3) to the whole world.

Returning to 2017:

In October 2011, I developed an informal summary of events to demonstrate that the issues I addressed in the first edition of this book were supported by the listed events; it is presented in Appendix A. I gave up adding to it after October 2011 upon realizing that the amount of supporting information was overwhelming. Here we are in 2017, and the current events of (1) the US's and Great Britain's simultaneous unraveling; (2) Russia's invasion of Ukraine, its movement into Syria, and its courting of the Iranians; and (3) the awakening of Asian military might and economic power fully support what I said in 2011. A simple perusal of press headlines bolsters my points.

Military Brass Sound Alarm about 'Insidious Decline' in [US Military] *Readiness*

http://www.foxnews.com/politics/2017/02/09/military-brass-sound-alarm-about-insidious-decline-in-readiness.html

Fox News, February 9, 2017

'Milestone' Agreement is Signed: China, Japan, and ROK [South Korea] *on Course for Landmark Regional Trade Pact*

China Daily, May 14, 2012

Video Shows Tens of Thousands Amassing at Turkey Border as Russia, Iran Bear Down on Key Syrian City

http://www.zerohedge.com/news/2016-02-05/video-shows-tens-thousands-massing-turkey-border-russia-iran-bear-down-key-syrian-ci

Zero Hedge, February 5, 2016

North Korea Moves up Window of Planned Rocket Launch

http://www.foxnews.com/world/2016/02/06/north-korea-moves-up-window-planned-rocket-launch.html?intcmp=hpbt3

Associated Press, February 6, 2016

North Korea Unites South Korea, Japan, and China: Three Neighbors Have Condemned its Test-firing of a Ballistic Missile

http://www.theamericanconservative.com/articles/north-korea-unites-south-korea-japan-and-china/

The American Conservative, September 12, 2016

A Eurasian Golden Triangle is Emerging with China, Russia and Iran as the Three Key Points, F. William Engdahl Notes

http://sputniknews.com/politics/20160203/1034171547/iran-china-russia-dollar.html

Sputnik News, February 3, 2016

China Warns Trump that Taiwan Policy is 'Non-Negotiable'

https://www.theguardian.com/us-news/2017/jan/15/china-warns-trump-that-taiwan-policy-is-non-negotiable

The Guardian, January 15, 2017

Iran to Buy More Russian Weapons, Foster Cooperation – Khamenei Aide

https://www.rt.com/news/331395-iran-russia-weapons-military/

Russian Times, February 5, 2016

Paul R. Wild

Russia Accuses Turkey of Preparing to Invade Syria

http://news.yahoo.com/russia-says-serious-grounds-suspect-turkey-preparing-invade-144435326.html

AFP, February 4, 2016

4 Reasons Russia and Turkey Can't Afford a Trade War

http://money.cnn.com/2015/11/26/news/turkey-russia-economy-trade-sanctions/

CNN Money, November 26, 2015

India's Economic Growth Accelerates: Gross Domestic Product Grows 7.4% Last Quarter

http://www.wsj.com/articles/indias-economic-growth-accelerates-1448886206

Wall Street Journal, November 30, 2015

US-India Defence Pact to Impact Pakistan, China

http://www.dawn.com/news/1280873/us-india-defence-pact-to-impact-pakistan-china

Dawn, Aug 30, 2016

How Much the World is Spending on Military: India is Number 4

http://www.ndtv.com/india-news/how-much-the-world-is-spending-on-military-india-is-number-4-1637643

NDTV, December 14, 2016

Asia's Top 5 Economies in 2030

http://nationalinterest.org/feature/asias-top-5-economies-2030-16898

The National Interest, July 8, 2016

Comment: The article above comments that, "Looking into the crystal ball, by 2030 Asia's top economies are expected to comprise China, India, Japan, Indonesia and South Korea...Could South Korea unite with the North?"

Even during the finishing stages of completing this book, the headlines above are outdated, considering North Korea's recent missile escapades and threats against the US, the brouhaha over Trump and the Russians, and on and on and on. Need I say more?

As a final point related to our destiny as a nation, there is an argument from logic, for which no supporting verses from Scripture can be identified clearly, that suggests we **must** be weakened and made of no consequence. Some students of prophecy state that, irrespective of whether or not the Bible has anything specific to say about the demise of the US, logically the US must be removed from power in order for the antichrist to arise. The US has stood as a bulwark against evil dominions for over 200 years, such that it is a reasonable argument to make that we must be neutralized to allow the ultimate, evil dominion of the antichrist to ascend to global dominance.

Is The United States Mentioned In Bible Prophecy?

Paul R. Wild

Good News

Doom and gloom. Is there any good news in all of this for US (us, *etc.*)? Absolutely, and it is exciting! For the last 42 years that I have studied prophecy, I have always believed that the US would suffer the general judgments that befall all nations leading up to the return of Christ. I had no hope for US. Now I do, and here's why: I now believe the picture of the lion-eagle being lifted up from the earth, made to stand up like a man, and being given the heart of a man represents *repentance and restoration*.

It is evident that in Scripture where God represents nations and peoples as beasts, there is nothing positive in the intent, in the same manner that Peter speaks of certain reprobate men as "natural brute beasts, made to be taken and destroyed." (2 Peter 2:12) From this, God's perspective is that the Anglo-American alliance is reprobate, depraved, and unreasoning. God deals harshly with it - its wings are plucked, suggesting that the wings themselves are removed from the lion or that the feathers are removed from the wings. In either case, it indicates judgment. By the absence of the wings on the amalgamated (part leopard, bear, and lion) Revelation 13:2 beast, which is the same as the beast with iron teeth, ten horns, and brass nails in Daniel 7:7,19, it suggests that the wings, meaning US, are completely removed, plucked from the body of the lion. On the other hand, the word used for plucked, "merat" (Strong's concordance 4804), is derived from "marat" (Strong's concordance 4803), which means "to polish or make bald," seemingly to indicate the wings remain but are stripped of their glorious plumage. Either we Americans are unceremoniously removed completely from shared influence with the Anglos, or we are thoroughly humiliated by having our feathers, our "glory" if you will, stripped to expose our nakedness.

We would not be the first nation that aligned itself with God only to sink into lawlessness, ultimately to have God "discover thy nakedness unto them, that they may see thy nakedness." (Ezekiel 16:37) Likewise, we would not be the first nation that has undergone national repentance after the Lord's chastening. My justification for speculating that either the US, the British, or both will undergo national repentance before the antichrist's kingdom overtakes the kingdoms of the other beasts is based on the language of the book of Daniel. It is always useful to look first in the book in which the riddle is posed.

Let us look at how certain key terms for our study are used in reference to Nebuchadnezzar. Daniel 4:16 states, "Let his heart be changed from man's, and let a beast's heart be given unto him...," meaning he was judged and degraded to the state of an unreasoning beast. But the lion-eagle beast will be upgraded to the opposite of what Nebuchadnezzar was degraded to: It will be made to stand upright like a man and will receive the heart of a man. It stands to reason that if Peter likens reprobate men to unreasoning beasts, then repentant men must be reasoning humans. Nebuchadnezzar was made to act and look like that to which God likened him, i.e., a beast, specifically an ox, an eagle, and a nondescript bird. Then, after a time of insanity, he was made to act in accordance with that to which God had restored him, i.e., human reason. He lifted up his eyes to heaven, after which his understanding returned to him and his glory was restored to him. That is the way it happens – repentance leads to enlightenment and restoration.

To further support the idea of repentance and restoration as our national destiny, the lion-eagle beast of Daniel 7 was lifted up from the earth, which is a picture of being raised up above the common and profane to an exalted or glorified state. Examination of the phrases "lifted up from the earth" and "high and lifted up," as used elsewhere in Scripture, such as Ezekiel 1:19,21; 10:16,19; Isaiah 6:1; and John 12:32, supports this idea of glorification:

*And I, if I be **lifted up from the earth**, will draw all men unto me.*

John 12:32

One is hard-pressed to see through natural eyes any glory in the lifting up of Christ on the cross, but seen through spiritual eyes it was glorious in its accomplishment of putting to death Death itself. Likewise, the picture of the lion-eagle beast being lifted up is one of glorification. I believe that one or both members of the Anglo-American alliance will achieve a greater glory based on spiritual renewal; we **will** recover our senses after a time of judgment, we **will** repent, and we **will** be restored. We will never recover our former glory in terms of financial and military might, but we **will** attain a greater glory as nations of Saints boldly declaring the Gospel of the Kingdom while patiently awaiting our King. This! Is! Good! News!

I cannot be dogmatic on the events postulated above for how the four beasts will operate in the last days, but I feel very strongly it is a probable scenario, and I feel even more strongly that the beasts of Daniel 7 are modern nations rather than those of antiquity. Therefore, it is safe to answer the question posed in the title in the affirmative, which is to say that **yes**, the US is mentioned in Bible prophecy. Consider this the opening salvo to a lively debate.

Paul R. Wild

THE EZEKIEL 38-39 AND PSALM 83 WARS

The timing of the Ezekiel 38 (and 39, hereinafter linked together as the Ezekiel 38-39 war) and Psalm 83 wars has long been a hotly-debated topic among students of prophecy. Some, such as Walid Shoebat and Joel Richardson, see them as Tribulation/Armageddon events, whereas others see them as pre-Tribulation events. If Russia is included as one of the nations of Ezekiel 38-39 that invades Israel but is soundly defeated, then it would be consistent with the position I have taken for Daniel 7 that Russia wanes in power and is succeeded by the Asians **before** the antichrist ascends to power.

In other words, the events of Psalm 83 and Ezekiel 38-39 are **before** the Tribulation, **not during** it. However, it can be very confusing and easy to interpret Ezekiel 38-39 as Tribulation events because there are numerous terms that are in common with terms used in Tribulation verses from Isaiah, Joel, Micah, Matthew, Luke, Revelation, etc. Ezekiel 38-39 speak of earthquakes, pestilence, nations knowing that God is the Lord, birds eating the flesh of men, Israel knowing that the Lord is their God, and on and on. These certainly have the ring of the Tribulation, particularly Armageddon which culminates in "the day of the Lord," the literal day when Christ returns to the earth to destroy all who oppose Him and those who seek to slaughter His people Israel. The "day of the Lord" is described or mentioned directly or indirectly in 48 passages of Scripture, and if we included passages that use the phrases "in that day" or "at that time," we likely could find many additional passages that speak of this day. A few passages are presented below to aid the reader in understanding this day, with the full 48 passages presented in Appendix B:

- **Isaiah 2:12**

For the day of the LORD of hosts shall be upon every one that is proud and lofty, and upon every one that is lifted up; and he shall be brought low:

- **Isaiah 13:6**

Howl ye; for the day of the LORD is at hand; it shall come as a destruction from the Almighty.

- **Isaiah 13:9**

Behold, the day of the LORD cometh, cruel both with wrath and fierce anger, to lay the land desolate: and he shall destroy the sinners thereof out of it.

- **Isaiah 34:8**

For it is the day of the LORD's vengeance, and the year of recompences for the controversy of Zion.

- **Jeremiah 46:10**

For this is the day of the Lord GOD of hosts, a day of vengeance, that he may avenge him of his adversaries: and the sword shall devour, and it shall be satiate and made drunk with their blood: for the Lord GOD of hosts hath a sacrifice in the north country by the river Euphrates.

- **Joel 1:15**

Alas for the day! for the day of the LORD is at hand, and as a destruction from the Almighty shall it come.

- **Joel 2:1**

Blow ye the trumpet in Zion, and sound an alarm in my holy mountain: let all the inhabitants of the land tremble: for the day of the LORD cometh, for it is nigh at hand;

- **Joel 2:11**

And the LORD shall utter his voice before his army: for his camp is very great: for he is strong that executeth his word: for the day of the LORD is great and very terrible; and who can abide it?

- **Joel 2:31**

The sun shall be turned into darkness, and the moon into blood, before the great and terrible day of the LORD come.

- **Joel 3:14**

Multitudes, multitudes in the valley of decision: for the day of the LORD is near in the valley of decision.

Nevertheless, even with some similar language between Ezekiel and the apocalyptic language of the Tribulation events and the Day of the Lord, there are many differences, as elucidated in the following:

1. **Israel is secure in Ezekiel 38 immediately prior to the attack by its enemies and will remain in the land, whereas during the Tribulation Israel will be on the run from the antichrist and hiding in Jordan.**

Israel is secure in Ezekiel 38, which will not be the case during the Tribulation, because Daniel 11:41 and Revelation 12:14, when linked, say Israel will flee to the wilderness for 3.5 years, and the antichrist will have rule over the earth during that time. Do not make the mistake that some do of equating peace with security. Some commentators maintain that Ezekiel 38:8, which says, "…they (Israel) will dwell safely all of them," means that at some future time the antichrist will make a false peace covenant with them, allowing Israel to be dwelling peacefully immediately before the antichrist betrays them. However, the key word is "safely," not peacefully. Israel is not now and will not be at peace, meaning free of conflict with its enemies, at the time of the Ezekiel 38 invasion, but it is now and will be living securely, or safely, at that time. Israel has a world-class defense system, and its people are well trained to repel invaders and have done so through at least seven major conflicts since 1948. But during the Ezekiel 38 invasion, they will be overwhelmed by the sheer enormity of the invading force, so God Himself will intervene to use geologic, climatologic, and epidemiologic disasters to destroy them. With respect to Israel's hasty departure from the land during the Tribulation, I postulate that they will flee to Jordan in the area of Bozrah (which means sheepfold, where the sheep are protected, and by some commentators equivalent to ancient Petra and Biblical Sela), on the basis of Isaiah 63:1 and Daniel 11:41:

Paul R. Wild

Who is this that cometh from Edom, with dyed garments from Bozrah? this that is glorious in his apparel, travelling in the greatness of his strength? I that speak in righteousness, mighty to save. [Jesus, who has returned to gather the hiding Jews]

Isaiah 63:1

He [the antichrist] *shall enter also into the glorious land, and many countries shall be overthrown: but these shall escape out of his hand, even Edom, and Moab, and the chief of the children of Ammon* [modern Jordan].

Daniel 11:41

I've seen this area with my own eyes and can attest to it being a great place to seek refuge away from an invading army by the dual virtues of the terrain and climate. I believe they will be able to flee to Jordan at the beginning of the 3.5-year Tribulation unobstructed by the Jordanians because the Jordanians will have been defeated earlier by Israel in the war described in Psalm 83 before the Tribulation. Psalm 83 is short but loaded with information, so I will present all of it here.

Keep not thou silence, O God: hold not thy peace, and be not still, O God. ² For, lo, thine enemies make a tumult: and they that hate thee have lifted up the head. ³ They have taken crafty counsel against thy people, and consulted against thy hidden ones. ⁴ They have said, Come, and let us cut them off from being a nation; that the name of Israel may be no more in remembrance. ⁵ For they have consulted together with one consent: they are confederate against thee: ⁶ The tabernacles of Edom, and the Ishmaelites; of Moab, and the Hagarenes; *⁷ Gebal, and Ammon, and Amalek; the Philistines with the inhabitants of Tyre; ⁸ Assur also is joined with them: they have holpen the children of Lot. Selah. ⁹ Do unto them as unto the Midianites; as to Sisera, as to Jabin, at the brook of Kison: ¹⁰ Which perished at Endor: they became as dung for the earth. ¹¹ Make their nobles like Oreb, and like Zeeb: yea, all their princes as Zebah, and as Zalmunna: ¹² Who said, Let us take to ourselves the houses of God in possession. ¹³ O my God, make them like a wheel; as the stubble before the wind. ¹⁴ As the fire burneth a wood, and as the flame setteth the mountains on fire; ¹⁵ So persecute them with thy tempest, and make them afraid with thy storm. ¹⁶ Fill their faces with shame; that they may seek thy name, O Lord. ¹⁷ Let them be confounded and troubled for ever; yea, let them be put to shame, and perish: ¹⁸ That men may know that thou, whose name alone is Jehovah, art the most high over all the earth.*

Psalm 83

In Psalm 83, Jordan is identified by "the tabernacles of Edom, and the Ishmaelites; of Moab, and the Hagarenes," wherein Edom and Moab were kingdoms within what is now Jordan; the Hagarenes indicate Egyptians; and the Ishmaelites indicate Arabs in a general sense. Gebal, also known as ancient Byblos, equates to Lebanon by virtue of its location about 25 miles north of modern Beirut; Ammon was another kingdom located in modern Jordan; Amalek was nomadic but was known to inhabit southern Israel and northern Egypt in the Negev Desert and might relate to the modern Gaza Strip inhabited by Palestinians; the Philistines may also relate to the

Gaza Strip but perhaps also to the Palestinian territories; Tyre is a Lebanese city; and Assur equates to modern Syria through geographic association with the "children of Lot" (Ammon and Moab), meaning Jordan, although it may also indicate Assyria, or modern Iraq. The modern equivalents of the invading nations of Ezekiel 38-39 are Russia; Iran; Turkey; perhaps other Muslim nations like Azerbaijan and the various "stans" that were once part of the old USSR; and Ethiopia, possibly including Sudan, based on the Greek historian Herodotus who considered anything south of Egypt as Ethiopia. These nations would have to go through the territories of the modern equivalents of the invading nations of Psalm 83 to get to Israel. Jordan, Lebanon, Syria, Gaza, Egypt, and the Palestinians are the nations of Psalm 83 that immediately surround Israel. For the nations of Ezekiel 38-39 to go through the nations of Psalm 83, it suggests that the nations of Psalm 83 either have been wiped out previously by the Israelis or by God Himself, or that the nations of Psalm 83 are working in collusion with the nations of Ezekiel 38-39 to destroy Israel. These nations could be working together generally by consensus or specifically through the mutual defense treaties that they have been enacting in recent years.

Perhaps the nations of Psalm 83 attack Israel first and are wiped out. I suspect that Israel's army will accomplish the destruction of the Psalm 83 nations because Psalm 83 references the Canaanites (Sisera and Jabin) and the Midianites (Oreb and Zeeb) who were defeated by Barak's and Gideon's Israelite armies - with the Lord's help, of course (Judges 4 and 7). The Psalm 83 war conceivably could be the event that causes Damascus to be "taken away from being a city, and it shall be a ruinous heap," in accordance with Isaiah 17:1. The devastation of those small nations then could incite the nations of Ezekiel 38-39 to attack, perhaps because of rage against Israel or simply because they will feel Israel is vulnerable and easily can be overthrown.

2. **The burial place of Gog of Ezekiel 38-39 and the burial place of the antichrist of the Tribulation are not the same.** Ezekiel 39:11 says Gog, whom Shoebat equates to an Islamic antichrist, will be buried east of Israel in Jordan, whereas Revelation 19:20 says the antichrist will be thrown directly into the lake of fire at the end of the Tribulation.

3. **The territorial boundaries of the land of Israel described in Ezekiel 38-39 are different than the territorial boundaries of the land of Israel after the Tribulation, meaning that the war of Ezekiel 38-39 cannot be equated to the Battle of Armageddon of the Tribulation.** I cannot be dogmatic about this, but I believe that to "cleanse the land" (Ezekiel 39:12) would necessitate burying the bodies of the invading hordes outside the land, which is what Ezekiel 39:11 suggests. Ezekiel 39:11 states that the Gog armies will have a burial place east of the sea, which is the Dead

Sea, and that area is currently not part of "the land" of Israel; the area east of the Dead Sea is modern Jordan. Some might argue that the sea could be the Mediterranean, meaning that a burial place "east of the sea" would place that area in Israel. However, it is necessary to look at clues that help to explain which sea is intended. For example, Ezekiel 27:32 uses "sea" in association with a seaside city (Tyre), which makes it clear the Mediterranean is intended. In Ezekiel 47:10 where there is no seaside city association, the term "great sea" is used to indicate the Mediterranean. With that in mind, where it is not obvious that the Mediterranean is intended as the "sea," then the Dead Sea is in view, as in Ezekiel 39:11. Furthermore, there are some commentators that make a compelling case that the place of burial and the nearby city, Hamonah (verse 39:16), are in modern Jordan. They argue that Hamonah will be the new name of the city that was called Dibon by the Moabites and ancient Israelites, now the modern city of Dhiban in Jordan.

If cleansing the land means burying the dead bodies outside the land of Israel, then it means burying them in Jordan. Why is this important for distinguishing the war of Ezekiel 38-39 from a Tribulation war? Well, the area where the bodies will be buried "outside the land" after the Ezekiel war will suddenly be "in the land" after the Tribulation war, also commonly referred to as the Battle of Armageddon. The land apportioned to the Israelis after

Armageddon and the return of Christ will suddenly *encompass* the burial area east of the sea, i.e., modern Jordan. How do I know this?

In Genesis 15:18-21, God told Abram (Abraham) that He would give Abram's descendants lands that they currently do not possess, basically taking all or part of modern Jordan, Egypt, Turkey, Syria, and Iraq, and possibly Saudi Arabia, Yemen, Qatar, and other nations along the Arabian Gulf. The Kenites, Kenizzites, and Kadmonites mentioned in Genesis 15 inhabited what became Edom, Ammon, and Moab, which are modern Jordan. Numbers 35:9-15, Deuteronomy 4:41-43 and 19:1-9, and Joshua 20 speak about cities of refuge, six of which were apportioned at the time Israel entered the Promised Land after their 40 years of wandering in the wilderness, and three of which will be apportioned during the millennial reign of Christ. Specifically, Israel's borders will be expanded after Christ's return to include three cities of refuge on the east side of the Jordan River in addition to the three that were on the east side and the three that were on the west side during the time of Joshua and the Judges.

To sum it up: If "cleanse the land" means to remove the dead from it, then it argues for "the land" being confined to Israel's **modern** borders and **not future** ones, meaning that the war of Ezekiel 38-39 is **pre-Tribulation, not Armageddon**, and **not immediately**

before the return of Christ to apportion the land to Israel during His millennial kingdom.

4. **The means and methods of the destruction of the Ezekiel 38-39 armies are different than those described for the destruction of the antichrist and his armies.** No mention is made of Christ and His armies coming back to deal directly with the armies of Ezekiel 38-39 or, for that matter, the armies of Psalm 83. God destroys the Ezekiel 38-39 armies indirectly through natural-appearing phenomena, such as an earthquake, torrential rain, hail, possible volcanic activity, and disease, which will be divinely controlled. This is unlike Joel 2, Isaiah 63, Zechariah 14, Revelation 19, and other passages wherein Christ and His armies directly are confronting the antichrist and his armies.

5. **The means and methods of Israel's physical restoration after the Ezekiel 38-39 war are different from those described for Israel's physical restoration after the Battle of Armageddon and the return of Christ.** Ezekiel 39:9-16 say the Israelis will burn the weapons for seven years and bury bodies for seven months, whereas immediately after Armageddon Jesus will restore the entire earth Himself. It seems highly unlikely that weapons burning and body burial will be occurring during the early stages of Christ's millennial reign. The earth's restoration after Christ's return is described in Ezekiel 47; Amos 9:11-15; Zechariah 14:5-11; Isaiah 2:1-4, 11:5, 65:25; and

Micah 4:1-5. Additionally, Daniel 12:11 hints at a period of judgment (perhaps the judgment of the nations that Jesus mentions in Matthew 25:31-46) and apportionment of the land among the 12 Tribes of Israel, specifically the 45-day period between day 1290 and day 1335 after the "abomination of desolation." If that is what is occurring during that period, it seemingly precludes the burning and burial activities mentioned in Ezekiel 39:9-16.

6. **The number of nations involved in the Ezekiel 38-39 war is significantly less than the number of nations involved in Armageddon; "all nations" will be gathered at Armageddon.** Revelation, Matthew, Mark, Luke, Zechariah, and others indicate that all nations will be gathered against Israel, but Ezekiel 38-39 indicate only a few, specific nations will attack Israel. Moreover, certain nations are specifically stated as non-participants in Gog's attack on Israel, namely "Sheba, and Dedan, and the merchants of Tarshish, with all the young lions thereof." Rather, these nations appear to protest or at least question Gog's invasion. See Point 11 below.

7. **The rationale for invasion described in Ezekiel 38-39 is different than the rationale for invasion described in Revelation.** The emphasis of Ezekiel 38-39 is to take spoil, whereas the Battle of Armageddon is to destroy Israel and wage war against Jesus as He returns to take control of the earth.

8. **The physiographic regions for the Ezekiel and Tribulation wars are different.** Ezekiel 38 says Gog will cover the mountains of Israel, whereas Armageddon's battleground is a valley, probably the Great Rift Valley, including the Jordan Rift Valley. The armies of the antichrist will gather in the Valley of Megiddo in northern Israel, also called by some the Valley of Jezreel, but will try to move into southern Jordan where the Israelis will be hiding in Bozrah. The antichrist will be unsuccessful, based on Daniel 11:41: "...but these shall escape out of his hand, even Edom, and Moab, and the chief of the children of Ammon" (modern Jordan). This valley system is elsewhere in Scripture called the winepress (Isaiah 63:1-6) and the valley of decision (Joel 3:14), where Jesus will tread to destroy these armies.

9. **The Ezekiel 38-39 war will likely pave the way for the building of the temple that will be defiled by the antichrist; his placement of the "abomination of desolation" in the temple is the event that initiates the Tribulation.** An unstated but implied reason for why the wars of Ezekiel and Revelation are not the same is one of reasonable deduction, i.e., an if/then statement related to what event transpires to allow the temple of Revelation 11:1-2 to be built. If the temple is to be built, then how can it be built unless the Jews have free access to the Temple Mount and Muslim edifices like the Dome of the Rock are removed? The war of Ezekiel 38-39 is likely the mechanism God will use to destroy the Dome of the

Rock on the Temple Mount in Jerusalem to allow the Revelation 11:1-2 temple to be built, and it is likely the event that sets up the global crisis that will make it conducive for a global leader to stand up to come up with a false peace plan.

10. **The reference in Ezekiel 39:2 to leaving one sixth of the armies alive from the Ezekiel 38-39 war indicates only a partial destruction of Gog's armies, whereas the Battle of Armageddon will result in complete and total annihilation of the antichrist and his armies.** The KJV uses the phrase "And I will turn thee back, and *leave but the sixth part of thee...*," in Ezekiel 39:2, whereas other versions use something akin to, "and I will turn you around and *lead you on...*" The Hebrew verb used in verse 39:2 is shawshaw, (שׁאשׁא, "drive") very similar in the original lettering to שׁשׁא, shashah, which are respectively Strong's concordance numbers 8338 and 8341. I will not be so bold to say that it doesn't exist elsewhere, but I cannot find the Hebrew verb שׁאשׁא (shawshaw, 8338, "drive") used anywhere else in the Bible; however, I can find שׁשׁה (shashah, 8341, "sixth") and its related nouns 8337 (shesh) and 8345 (shishee), all relating to six or sixth. With reference to 8338, Strong's defines it by saying, "A primary root; apparently, to annihilate -- leave by the sixth part (by confusion with 8341)."

There are several other words in Hebrew that mean lead, drive, or drag, depending upon which English translation is consulted, so it is interesting to note that none of those Hebrew words is used in Ezekiel 39:2. The point I am making here is that God did not inspire Ezekiel to use a word that absolutely means lead, drag, or drive but instead inspired him to use a word that seems to indicate an action against something like leading, driving, or dragging to the point that only one sixth of it is left. Shawshaw, 8338, appears to blend two ideas. As alluded to by Strong's definition, there are some commentators who believe the way 8338 is translated in the KJV indicates that the KJV translators understood the word to be used as a colloquialism in the way we use "decimate" to stand for complete annihilation of something. In reality, the Latin root for the word decimate comes from the Roman practice of taking 1/10 of their own armies that were defeated and killing them as a form of punishment for failure. In the same way, these commentators believe that 8338 over time became used to mean, essentially, judgment by leaving but a sixth. Therefore, I believe the KJV is correct and demonstrates an understanding that the KJV translators had of the context of Ezekiel 38-39.

More directly stated, I believe a portion of the invading armies of Ezekiel 38-39 must be left behind in order to have some of their armies remaining to participate in the final war over Israel, i.e., Revelation's Battle of Armageddon and Daniel's final war of Daniel 11:35-45. The KJV translation of shawshaw as "leave but the sixth part" rather than "drive" would then support the idea that the invasion of Ezekiel 38-39 is a pre-Tribulation event.

11. **The way the words Tarshish, Sheba, and Dedan are used in Ezekiel 38:13 indicates that not all nations will be involved in the Ezekiel 38-39 war, whereas the Battle of Armageddon will involve all nations.** Shoebat and Richardson maintain that Gog is the antichrist of Turkish origin and that Tarshish is Tarsus of Biblical times and also the modern city of Tarsus in Turkey. They do not believe that Tarshish is a reference to a far-western city, such as ancient Tartessos in Spain or perhaps a city in the British Isles. They argue that the Bible is Middle Eastern-centric, so that place names follow suit, meaning that Tarshish is a Middle-Eastern city. Another argument they make is that the precious metals associated with Tarshish were mined in the Taurus Mountains north of Tarsus.

The argument against Shoebat's and Richardson's position is that it is known that Tartessos in Spain also had abundant precious metals through trade, as recorded by Greek historians. 1 Kings 10:19 indicates that ships of Tarshish came every three years to Israel during the time of Solomon, suggesting a much more distant location than that of Tarsus, which is less than 300 nautical miles from the ancient Israelite port of Joppa, from where Jonah tried to flee from God. Furthermore, in Ezekiel 38:13, "Sheba, and Dedan, and the merchants of Tarshish, with all the young lions thereof shall say unto thee, Art thou come to take a spoil?," suggesting that they are not part of this war and appear to be protesting. Sheba and Dedan are generally understood by commentators to indicate Arabic peoples, probably modern Saudi Arabia and possibly other Arabian Gulf States, such as Qatar, UAE, Kuwait, etc. "The young lions thereof" are believed by many commentators to be a reference to nations emanating from the former British Empire (the lion of Daniel 7) or nations from Western Europe in general, including countries of the Americas. To support my contention that Saudi Arabia will not be participating in the invasion of Israel, consider this relatively recent headline:

US Concerned as Saudi Arabia, Israel Team Up Against Common Foe Iran

http://atimes.com/2015/09/us-concerned-as-saudi-arabia-israel-move-closer-to-thwart-iran/

Asia Times News & Features, September 9, 2015

If Tarshish is meant to be a city in Turkey, and if Gog is meant to be a Turkish antichrist leading Turkish Islamic armies, then why would the merchants of Tarshish question their own leader in unison with Arab nations? Would that not be grounds for getting one's head cut off? The Saudi government in particular has not had the same level of animus toward Israel as other Arab nations and was exposed in recent years by Wikileaks as offering the Israelis safe air passage to bomb Iran's nuclear research and development facilities. Given that the events of the Tribulation described in Revelation strongly appear to be global, and that the context of Isaiah 66, and Isaiah 66:16,18 in particular, indicate that "all flesh" and "all nations and tongues" will be involved, then how could these nations be excluded from those which participate in the Battle of Armageddon unless Armageddon is not what is described in Ezekiel 38-39?

12. **Ezekiel 38-39 indicate that Israel and many nations will know in a general sense that God is protecting Israel, but they do not indicate unequivocally that these nations will know specifically that Jesus Christ is that God Who is protecting Israel. This is in stark contrast to the passages regarding the Tribulation that make it crystal clear that all the nations will know Who He is when He returns to destroy the antichrist and save Israel.** Those who believe that Ezekiel's war is a Tribulation event cite the fact that both the heathens and the house of Israel will "know" God and know that He is in the land, in other words a reference to Christ's physical return to Israel.

I believe that the word "know" refers to a general sense of knowing that the God of the Bible was divinely protecting Israel to accomplish such a massive blow against Gog and his armies, but that it will not result in them specifically knowing their

Messiah. I suspect that it will cause a significant number of Muslims and others to re-evaluate their theologies. Perhaps it will cause billions around the globe to be more open to the concept of a nondescript god that involves himself with the affairs of men, causing the lost sea of humanity to feel a spiritual vacuum into which the antichrist will step. On the other hand, it will also likely cause some among both Jews and Gentiles to place their faith in Christ. Nevertheless, I believe the majority of Jews will still not be able to connect the dots back to Jesus Christ.

I postulate that all the events after Ezekiel 38-39's war will be the means by which the antichrist will manipulate the world by aligning himself with Israel and convincing the world that Israel is unique and should be allowed to build their temple. He will "confirm" the seven-year covenant, which I believe may be a resurrected Oslo Peace Accords that was never fully implemented, to allow the temple's construction and then present himself as the Messiah at the midpoint of the covenant period, marking the beginning of the 3.5-year Tribulation. The non-elect (in contrast to the elect that Jesus discusses in Matthew 24:24) will easily be deceived into thinking the antichrist is God and will follow him to eternal destruction. Only at the end of the Tribulation will the Jews look upon Him Whom they pierced and recognize their Messiah (Zechariah 12:10), and then all Israel will be saved (Romans 11:26). The whole world of unbelievers will recognize Him and will wage war against Him as He returns in glory with His Bride (Revelation 19:11-21).

13. **Gog is a nation, not a man, and the reference in Revelation to Gog leading a revolt at the end of the millennial reign of Christ indicates Gog cannot be the antichrist leading the attack on Israel in Ezekiel 38-39.** The prophetical Gog is mentioned in only two books of Scripture, Ezekiel and Revelation. Shoebat states that the Gog of Ezekiel is the antichrist, but this would then make him the Gog of Revelation 20:8 who gathers the armies of the earth to make a final attack on Jerusalem where Christ has been reigning for 1,000 years. The flaw in Shoebat's argument is that the antichrist is occupied elsewhere at the end of Christ's millennial reign:

And the devil that deceived them [i.e., Gog, Magog, and the other nations with them] *was cast into the lake of fire and brimstone, where the beast and the false prophet are, and shall be tormented day and night for ever and ever.*

Revelation 20:10

Based on the usage of Gog in Revelation, the Gog of Ezekiel cannot be identified as the antichrist and should be identified as a nation of preeminence among its allies rather than as a human leader. This is not an uncommon feature of Scripture wherein the titular head of a nation is used to identify an entire nation. See for yourself by examining the uses of Israel, Asshur, Mizraim, Ammon, Moab, Ephraim, Judah, Canaan, and on and on and on.

14. **In spite of the absence of numerous references to Gog in Scripture but numerous references to the antichrist, the weight of evidence favors Gog being a nation and not another name for the antichrist.** Shoebat believes that the question posed to Gog in Ezekiel 38:17, "...Art thou he of whom I have spoken in old time by my servants the prophets of Israel, which prophesied in those days many years that I would bring thee against them?," must mean that Gog is the antichrist. Shoebat argues that only the antichrist was consistently prophesied about by the prophets of Israel regarding Israel's future devastation, so that no other person fits the description. Admittedly, that is a good point, because there are numerous prophecies of the antichrist in the Old Testament, but I am hard pressed to find other, clear prophecies of Gog, other than Revelation 20:8. Perhaps he (or it, if it is a nation, as I believe) was prophesied about in the oral tradition of Israel but not recorded in the sacred writings. There are other examples of events referenced once in Scripture but not referenced elsewhere. For instance, Hebrews 11 references among the heroes of faith someone who was sawn asunder, but we do not know who that was, though many believe it to have been Isaiah. Perhaps Gog was prophesied about in a general sense as a representative of any number of unnamed pagan nations that would invade the land to destroy Israel. One commentator believes God's question to Gog is sarcastic and rhetorical in order to downplay Gog's

significance, the answer to the question being, "No," that Gog is not in the same league as the antichrist who was prophesied about many times in the Old Testament. I do not have an ironclad response to Shoebat's position, but suffice it to say that the weight of evidence presented above is in favor of Gog being someone or something other than the antichrist.

APPENDIX A - RECENT EVENTS SINCE JUNE 2011

October 11, 2011

This document is a companion piece to the "US in Prophecy" paper and is intended to demonstrate current events that support the major points of the paper, specifically that (1) the United States is waning in power and influence while the Russians and Asians, in particular the Chinese, are gaining in power and influence, and that (2) the stage is being set for the wars of Psalm 83 and Ezekiel 38.

US Decline

Russian Advancements

1. Rosneft (Russia Petroleum) buying select ExxonMobil Gulf of Mexico and onshore assets. Rosneft is owned by the Russian government, meaning Russia has authority over US soil.

2. On 8/2/11, Russian PM Putin declares, "...the US is a parasite on the world economy because of their monopoly of the dollar."

3. Russia is continuing to make progress toward joining the World Trade Organization.

Chinese Advancements

4. China is buying huge parcels of land in US, meaning China has authority over US soil. China is making a bid for the Los Angeles Dodgers.

5. Chemical & Engineering News reports in 8/29/11 edition: "The ease of setting up drug companies in China is starting to make the US appear less attractive."

6. Fox News online reports on 9/20/11 that California industry representatives are angry that China produced most of the steel for the new San Francisco-Oakland Bay Bridge, while CalDOT officials say they saved $400m by avoiding US union wages and benefits.

7. Environmental Protection News reports "China Makes U.S. Green Tech Companies an Offer They Can't Refuse. Invest in China now. China's economic rise already has the United States shaking in our boots, and they're about to deliver their K-O punch by emerging as the global leader in green technology."

Decaying Economy

8. Moneynews reports US competitiveness drops for third year straight.

9. The US Postal Service is threatening bankruptcy and declares its intention to significantly downsize its work force and services.

10. Bank of America is proposing to lay off 40,000 people. Moody's Investors Service has lowered Bank of America Corp.'s debt ratings, saying it is now less likely that the U.S. government would step in and prevent the lender from failing in a crisis.

11. Chase Bank still has high (meaning bad) troubled asset ratio. Banking industry in general unhealthy.

12. On 9/15, the director of Standard & Poors stated that there is a 1 in 3 chance of another US credit worthiness downgrade by 2012/2013.

13. The Department of Labor reports no new jobs in August, sending the Dow plummeting over 250 points on September 2. NYT reports one expert saying it may take four years to recover jobs to pre-recession levels.

14. US solar panel manufacturer, Solyndra, goes bankrupt even after $535 M loan from the Obama administration, citing inability to compete with Chinese solar panels.

15. Conservative Action Alerts reports General Electric (GE) closed its last incandescent light bulb factory in Winchester, Virginia, because the legislation that Congress passed in 2007 phases out and bans traditional light bulbs by 2015. GE told its employees that because it would be too expensive to retrofit its U.S. factories to make the labor-intensive CFLs and LEDs, the company had to lay off its American employees and move its factories to China and Mexico. Workers at the Winchester factory offered to take cuts in pay and benefits if they could keep their jobs, but GE declined that offer.

Cultural Decay

16. Black youths conduct a mass attack on white patrons at Wisconsin State Fair. Black youths instigate flash mobs in Philadelphia, Chicago, and other cities, beating up pedestrians and looting stores. White youths in Mississippi randomly pick a black man for harassment, beat him severely, and then run him over.

17. A football game between a Texas high school and a Mexican high school is called off because drug cartels were demanding $30,000 from the Mexican team to be allowed to play.

18. Students as young as those in the fifth grade in Washington, DC's public schools will soon be surveyed about their knowledge of sex, contraceptives, and drug use.

19. Students at Columbia University say they were "excited" about the prospect of dining with one of the world's most brutal chief executives, Iranian president Mahmoud Ahmadinejad. Scheduled to speak on 23 September 2011 at his fifth United Nations (UN) General Assembly appearance, Ahmadinejad had somehow been permitted to invite Columbia student members of a group called CIRCA, the Columbia International Relations Council and Association, to a private dinner. When threatened with civil and criminal legal action by the Israel Law Center, Columbia president Lee C.

Bollinger hastened to clarify that the event would not be held on campus.

20. Media Research Center reports that left-wing billionaire George Soros is funding a course at Washington State University called "Covering Islam in America" that teaches journalists how to downplay the negative aspects of Islam.

21. Halal Advocates, a Muslim advocacy group, reports in July that Costco is now selling halal meats, or Islamic "holy" meat. The ritual involves facing Mecca and the black stone that is worshipped there while killing the animal and crying out "Allah akbar," in essence making it meat sacrificed to an idol, the eating of which the Apostle Paul prohibited, as described in 1 Corinthians.

22. In July, the Austin American Statesman reports that "A Turkish group with possible connections to a growing charter school system that has raised eyebrows among some conservative state lawmakers is working with the Austin school district on a Turkish language program at a handful of Austin schools." The group is associated with the Harmony Science schools, which is a front organization that indoctrinates children into Muslim concepts and which is headed by Fethullah Gulen, an Islamist behind the resurgence of Islam in Turkey. The charter schools are funded by American tax dollars.

Sense of Impending Doom

23. Pastor of First Baptist Dallas preaches on tenth anniversary of 9/11 that the end of the US is inevitable.

24. Christian patriot groups all over US preparing for worst. Survivalist web sites and blogs going exponential. Weapons, ammo, and survivalist gear sales increasing in like manner.

Natural Disasters

25. Earthquake in unusual US place: Virginia. Drought and wildfires in Texas. Flooding in Pennsylvania, Maryland, Iowa, Nebraska, Louisiana. Hurricanes and Tropical storms on East and Gulf Coasts. Natural disasters are not unusual, but the economic burden will tax the economy more drastically now than during good economic times. Fox reported that costs of damage from tornadoes this year is roughly 3 times normal.

Political Disasters, Governmental Corruption, Governmental Tyranny

26. On 9/24, Danny Danon, a member of the Knesset confirmed on Huckabee (Fox) that Obama is pressuring Netanyahu to concede to Palestinian demands while publicly stating he is opposed to Palestinian statehood.

27. AG Eric Holder implicated in ATF's Operation Fast and Furious. ATF sold guns to Mexican drug gangs that used them to commit crimes against US citizens,

including murders of US agents. ATF field agents were not permitted to make arrests but were told to "stand down" by superiors.

28. By Executive Order in July, Obama directs federal agents to selectively enforce immigration laws. The Obama administration memo from the John Morton, Director of I.C.E. (Immigration and Customs Enforcement) directs I.C.E. agents now to use "prosecutorial discretion" with regard to enforcing immigration laws. Director Morton says that Obama Administration policy directs border patrol agents not to enforce immigration laws: "When ICE favorably exercises prosecutorial discretion, it essentially decides not to assert the full scope of the enforcement authority available to the agency." Obama's refusal to enforce immigration laws and opposition to AZ and AL's immigration laws are believed by political opponents to be Obama's and Democrat's plan to gain votes to ensure continued power for Democrats in Washington.

29. Obama has expressed support for the UN Small Arms Treaty, believed by many conservative watchdog groups to be an attempt to do an end around the Second Amendment. Conservative groups accuse Obama of using the Fast and Furious ATF scandal as an excuse to enact laws to further restrict private gun ownership.

30. On November 20, the Federal Communications Commission (FCC) will unconstitutionally seize

control of the Internet through their Net Neutrality regulations, bypassing Congress. Having granted itself the authority to regulate the Internet, the FCC has already begun strong-arming Internet Providers into supporting Net Neutrality guidelines on themselves or risk FCC imposed penalties. As a result, we are beginning to see early signs of what awaits religious and politically conservative websites. Web-hosting companies are starting to suspend these websites --classifying them as "hate sites." According to a Sept. 15, 2011 article in the Washington Times, Internet media giants aren't giving Christian and other faith-based groups a fair shake. Unless grassroots Americans rise up and challenge this federal power-grab, and demand Congress protect First Amendment free speech rights on the Internet, conservatives can and likely will be effectively silenced - removing the last hurdle for a radical socialist agenda to be implemented in our nation. "The FCC is not Congress. We cannot make laws," said Republican Commissioner Robert M. McDowell. "Some are saying that instead of acting as a cop on the beat, the FCC looks more like a regulatory vigilante." Republican Commissioner Meredith Atwell Baker was more direct, saying "Respectfully, I really, really, really dissent." She accused the FCC of acting simply to fulfill an Obama campaign promise to enact net neutrality rules. Their objections have been echoed by key congressional Republicans, who have warned the

FCC not to pass any net neutrality regulations and have promised hearings on the actions early next year. "Today, the Obama administration, which has already nationalized health care, the auto industry, insurance companies, banks and student loans, will move forward with what could be a first step in controlling how Americans use the Internet by establishing federal regulations on its use," Senate Minority Leader Mitch McConnell (R-Ken.) said Tuesday. "This would harm investment, stifle innovation, and lead to job losses. And that's why I, along with several of my colleagues, have urged the FCC chairman to abandon this flawed approach. The Internet is an invaluable resource. It should be left alone."

31. On 10/6, Senate Majority Leader Harry Reid (D-Nev.) triggered a rarely used procedural option informally called the "nuclear option" to change the Senate rules. Reid and 50 members of his caucus voted to change Senate rules unilaterally to prevent Republicans from forcing votes on uncomfortable amendments after the chamber has voted to move to final passage of a bill. Using a simple majority vote, Reid used the "Nuclear Option" to change the rules of the Senate so senators cannot offer amendments. In the future, senators will only be able to modify legislation if Harry Reid agrees to it. Harry Reid changed the rules of the Senate because Republicans planned to force a vote on President Obama's stimulus plan. The plan is so unpopular that it was

going to be defeated by Republicans and Democrats when it came up for a vote. This would have embarrassed the president so Reid and the Democrats just changed the longstanding rules of the Senate to block it.

32. Conservative Action Alerts has reported that the CDC is calling citizens' private phone numbers and intimidating them into providing their private medical records to check immunizations. CDC uses the term *vaccine immunization compliance* to imply that vaccines are required by law. The CDC checks what the citizens report by phone versus what the records report. Constitutionalist groups deem this another invasion of privacy by a government agency. This continues the trend into government intrusion and rejection of long-held Constitution interpretation, such as that a search warrant or the permission of the owner was required for the police before being allowed to enter a person's home. In an 8-1 decision on May 16, the Supreme Court of the United States swept that away. Now, according to the U.S. Supreme Court, police may enter a home if and when they "hear sounds suggesting evidence is being destroyed." Under the guise of the War on Drugs and War on Terror, authorities have long sought to expand their powers within the bounds of existing law. Between 2007 and 2009, the use of "delayed-notice" search warrants, or "sneak and peak" warrants, has grown from 700 to nearly 2,000 annually. With delayed-notice warrants, federal

agents are allowed to enter a home without the knowledge of the owner and search through the person's belongings. Although use of these special warrants has spiked since the renewal of the Patriot Act in 2005, information from the U.S. Justice Department shows the majority of them have been used in drug cases. The Court had also previously eroded conventional interpretation of the Constitution's Fifth Amendment with the Kelo case in 2005, wherein the decision of the Supreme Court allowed the city of New London, CT, to take private property not for public use, but for the private use of the New London Development Corporation to generate tax revenue.

33. The Obama administration in September instructed the Department of Defense to allow chaplains to marry same-sex couples. A coalition of 2,300 Christian chaplains from Catholic and Protestant backgrounds has stated to the Pentagon that they will not perform same-sex marriages.

Psalm 83/Middle East War

1. Egyptians over-run Israeli embassy in Cairo. Israelis flee.

2. Israel moves warships to Red Sea. Iran moves warships to Red Sea.

3. Palestinians use Egypt as passage for making incursions into southern Israel and killing Israeli citizens.

4. Libya falls to Islamists.

5. Syria under severe strain from Islamists.

6. Islamists take to the streets in protest in Amman, Jordan. The Islamist movement under the authority of the Muslim Brotherhood is growing.

7. Turkey breaks off diplomatic ties with Israel and kicks out Israeli ambassador. Turkey arrests the last vestiges of the military supporters of a secular government and is now an Islamic regime.

8. Turkey says it will arm its aid flotilla in case the Israelis try to board their ships like they did a couple years back.

9. Palestinian Authority seeks statehood through the UN, bypassing Israel and the Oslo Accords. PA threatens to unilaterally declare itself a state and threatens reprisals if Israel backs away from Oslo Accords, even though the PA routinely violates them, including having a security force nearly double what is allowed by the accords and prohibiting access to Jewish and Christian holy sites.

10. Hezbollah rises to dominance in Lebanese cabinet, giving more influence to Syria and Iran. All three nations have sworn to wipe out Israel.

11. Fox News reports on Tuesday, 9/20, that sanctions by the UN Security Council against Syria for its recent killings of civilian protesters have been held up because Russia is reluctant to call for sanctions

against "its ally." Russia and China veto sanctions against Syria on 10/4.

12. CIA Director Leon Panetta states on 10/3/11 that Israel is becoming increasingly isolated.

13. Canada's Globe and Mail reports on 10/4/11 that Turkey is increasingly deferring to conservative Muslim values, conducting purges of open air eateries in Istanbul that serve alcohol. "The problem is bigger than the tables and chairs," said Aydin Ali Kalayci, an executive member of Beydar, who runs a popular restaurant. "The problem is that the money is flowing now from the Middle East, so they want to make changes in our society. Time is running out for us."

14. This occurred before June 2011 but was just reported to me in October. On 4/2/11, Asia Time online reported: "Two diplomatic sources at the United Nations independently confirmed that Washington, via Secretary of State Hillary Clinton, gave the go-ahead for Saudi Arabia to invade Bahrain and crush the pro-democracy movement in their neighbor in exchange for a "yes" vote by the Arab League for a no-fly zone over Libya - the main rationale that led to United Nations Security Council resolution 1973."

Is The United States Mentioned In Bible Prophecy?

APPENDIX B – DAY OF THE LORD

1. Job 21:30

   *That the wicked is reserved to the **day** of destruction? they shall be brought forth to the day of wrath.*

2. Psalm 110:5

   *The Lord at thy right hand shall strike through kings in the **day** of his wrath.*

3. Proverbs 11:4

   *Riches profit not in the **day** of wrath: but righteousness delivereth from death.*

4. Isaiah 2:12

   *For the **day of the Lord** of hosts shall be upon every one that is proud and lofty, and upon every one that is lifted up; and he shall be brought low:*

5. Isaiah 13:6

   *Howl ye; for the **day of the Lord** is at hand; it shall come as a destruction from the Almighty.*

6. Isaiah 13:9

   *Behold, the **day of the Lord** cometh, cruel both with wrath and fierce anger, to lay the land desolate: and he shall destroy the sinners thereof out of it.*

7. Isaiah 13:13

   *Therefore I will shake the heavens, and the earth shall remove out of her place, in the wrath of the Lord of hosts, and in the **day** of his fierce anger.*

8. Isaiah 34:8

   *For it is the **day of the Lord's** vengeance, and the year of recompences for the controversy of Zion.*

9. Isaiah 63:4

   *For the **day** of vengeance is in mine heart, and the year of my redeemed is come.*

10. Jeremiah 46:10

    *For this is the **day of the Lord God** of hosts, a **day** of vengeance, that he may avenge him of his adversaries: and the sword shall devour, and it shall be satiate and made drunk with their blood: for the Lord GOD of hosts hath a sacrifice in the north country by the river Euphrates.*

11. Lamentations 2:22

    *Thou hast called as in a solemn **day** my terrors round about, so that in the **day of the Lord's** anger none escaped nor remained: those that I have swaddled and brought up hath mine enemy consumed.*

12. Ezekiel 7:19

    *They shall cast their silver in the streets, and their gold shall be removed: their silver and their gold shall not be able to deliver them in the **day of the wrath of the Lord**: they shall* *not satisfy their souls, neither fill their bowels: because it is the stumblingblock of their iniquity.*

13. Ezekiel 13:5

*Ye have not gone up into the gaps, neither made up the hedge for the house of Israel to stand in the battle in the **day of the Lord**.*

14. Ezekiel 30:3

*For the **day** is near, even the **day of the Lord** is near, a cloudy day; it shall be the time of the heathen.*

15. Ezekiel 38:19

*For in my jealousy and in the fire of my wrath have I spoken, Surely in that **day** there shall be a great shaking in the land of Israel;*

16. Joel 1:15

*Alas for the day! for the **day of the Lord** is at hand, and as a destruction from the Almighty shall it come.*

17. Joel 2:1

*Blow ye the trumpet in Zion, and sound an alarm in my holy mountain: let all the inhabitants of the land tremble: for the **day of the Lord** cometh, for it is nigh at hand;*

18. Joel 2:11

*And the LORD shall utter his voice before his army: for his camp is very great: for he is strong that executeth his word: for the **day of the Lord** is great and very terrible; and who can abide it?*

19. Joel 2:31

*The sun shall be turned into darkness, and the moon into blood, before the great and terrible **day of the Lord** come.*

20. Joel 3:14

*Multitudes, multitudes in the valley of decision: for the **day of the Lord** is near in the valley of decision.*

21. Amos 5:18

*Woe unto you that desire the day of the LORD! to what end is it for you? the **day of the Lord** is darkness, and not light.*

22. Amos 5:20

*Shall not the **day of the Lord** be darkness, and not light? even very dark, and no brightness in it?*

23. Obadiah 1:15

*For the **day of the Lord** is near upon all the heathen: as thou hast done, it shall be done unto thee: thy reward shall return upon thine own head.*

24. Nahum 1:7

*The Lord is good, a strong hold in the **day** of trouble; and he knoweth them that trust in him.*

25. Habakkuk 3:16

*When I heard, my belly trembled; my lips quivered at the voice: rottenness entered into my bones, and I trembled in myself, that I might rest in the **day** of trouble: when he cometh up unto the people, he will invade them with his troops.*

26. Zephaniah 1:7

*Hold thy peace at the presence of the Lord GOD: for the **day of the Lord** is at hand: for the LORD hath prepared a sacrifice, he hath bid his guests.*

27. Zephaniah 1:8

*And it shall come to pass in the **day of the Lord's** sacrifice, that I will punish the princes, and the king's children, and all such as are clothed with strange apparel.*

28. Zephaniah 1:14

*The great **day of the Lord** is near, it is near, and hasteth greatly, even the voice of the day of the LORD: the mighty man shall cry there bitterly.*

29. Zephaniah 1:15

*That **day** is a **day** of wrath, a **day** of trouble and distress, a **day** of wasteness and desolation, a **day** of darkness and gloominess, a **day** of clouds and thick darkness,*

30. Zephaniah 1:18

*Neither their silver nor their gold shall be able to deliver them in the **day of the Lord's** wrath; but the whole land shall be devoured by the fire of his jealousy: for he shall make even a speedy riddance of all them that dwell in the land.*

31. Zephaniah 2:2

*Before the decree bring forth, before the day pass as the chaff, before the fierce anger of the LORD come upon you, before the **day of the Lord's** anger come upon you.*

32. Zephaniah 2:3

*Seek ye the LORD, all ye meek of the earth, which have wrought his judgment; seek righteousness, seek meekness: it may be ye shall be hid in the **day of the Lord's** anger.*

33. Zechariah 14:1

*Behold, the **day of the Lord** cometh, and thy spoil shall be divided in the midst of thee.*

34. Malachi 4:5

*Behold, I will send you Elijah the prophet before the coming of the great and dreadful **day of the Lord**:*

35. Acts 2:20

*The sun shall be turned into darkness, and the moon into blood, before the great and notable **day of the Lord** come:*

36. Romans 2:5

*But after thy hardness and impenitent heart treasurest up unto thyself wrath against the **day of** wrath and revelation of the righteous judgment of God;*

37. 1 Corinthians 1:8*

*Who shall also confirm you unto the end, that ye may be blameless in the **day of our Lord Jesus Christ**.*

38. 1 Corinthians 5:5*

*To deliver such an one unto Satan for the destruction of the flesh, that the spirit may be saved in the **day of the Lord Jesus**.*

39. 2 Corinthians 1:14*

*As also ye have acknowledged us in part, that we are your rejoicing, even as ye also are ours in the **day of the Lord Jesus**.*

40. Philippians 1:6*

*Being confident of this very thing, that he which hath begun a good work in you will perform it until the **day of Jesus Christ**:*

41. Philippians 1:10*

*That ye may approve things that are excellent; that ye may be sincere and without offence till the **day of Christ**.*

42. 1 Thessalonians 5:2

*For yourselves know perfectly that the **day of the Lord** so cometh as a thief in the night.*

43. 2 Thessalonians 1:10

*When he shall come to be glorified in his saints, and to be admired in all them that believe (because our testimony among you was believed) in that **day**.*

44. 2 Thessalonians 2:2*

*That ye be not soon shaken in mind, or be troubled, neither by spirit, nor by word, nor by letter as from us, as that the **day of Christ** is at hand.*

45. 2 Thessalonians 2:3

*Let no man deceive you by any means: for that **day** shall not come, except there come a falling away first, and that man of sin be revealed, the son of perdition;*

46. 2 Peter 3:10

*But the **day of the Lord** will come as a thief in the night; in the which the heavens shall pass away with a great noise, and the elements shall melt with fervent heat, the earth also and the works that are therein shall be burned up.*

47. Hebrews 10:25

*Not forsaking the assembling of ourselves together, as the manner of some is; but exhorting one another: and so much the more, as ye see the **day** approaching.*

48. Revelation 6:17

*For the great **day** of his wrath is come; and who shall be able to stand?*

* Some commentators distinguish between "the day of the Lord" and "the day of our Lord Jesus Christ/Lord Jesus/Jesus Christ/Christ," stating that the contexts of the latter phrases are ones of hope, expectation, and reward for believers as opposed to the contexts of the former phrase as ones of wrath and destruction for unbelievers. Further study is needed to evaluate this distinction.

www.ingramcontent.com/pod-product-compliance
Lightning Source LLC
Chambersburg PA
CBHW070632300426
44113CB00010B/1750